Specimen of
Arnold Bennett's
handwriting in a
letter to his wife.

To Herman
many happy returns
of his ♪♪th birthday
November 4th. 1931
from

Jack Anderson

A

MY ARNOLD BENNETT

My favourite portrait of my husband.

MY ARNOLD BENNETT

By

MARGUERITE, HIS WIFE

IVOR NICHOLSON & WATSON, LTD.

44 ESSEX STREET
LONDON

First published 1931

Printed in Great Britain at
The Westminster Press
411A Harrow Road
London W.9

CONTENTS

CONTENTS

PROLOGUE

Iᴛ has been said about my husband that he loved punctuality. He did. He was suspicious of people who were not punctual. When he made an appointment he was always in fear one would be late.

He was convinced, at the time I met him, that no French people could be punctual, certainly no French woman, living in Paris, could be. I proved to him that French girls could make themselves do what they wished, when they had chosen to do so, even to being punctual. He loved people who kept their word. Not to be punctual for a rendezvous was not only an offence, it was a crime.

He had no patience with those who did not keep their word, even in minor things, while he was astonishingly patient to those calling on his patience, to endure what he openly objected to. He was extremely easy to please or displease; he had the gift of hiding his feelings marvellously well.

There was no placidity in him. He loved life far too much for possessing such a blessing. He had a feeble dose of inborn self-control and tact, for he was impulsive. He acquired both self-control and tact to a high degree as time went on. He knew what he wanted and what he was after. He was punctually exact, exacting and very tidy.

He did not like arguing; he loved to let others expose their ideas. He was occasionally surprised at their deeds. What was considered the wrong thing to do was not always found so by him. Good deeds from self-sacrificing natures would often meet with his entire disapproval. He believed in making use of his own life. Sentimentality, handicapping one, was to be swept away. He loved to see people acting from common sense chiefly, and not from moral or religious laws exclusively. He loved freedom for himself and for others. He preached freedom and common sense. People with moral courage and convictions appealed to him, others interested him. I guessed so much when I first knew him. Being an artist, he could not be otherwise.

It was the man in him I provoked when he claimed one day, in front of some friends and myself, that no woman could be punctual . . . that few men could be. We were listening to him. He went on. "I would not dream, for instance, of asking any of my friends to see me off when I go to Italy. They would be sure to be late. Besides, who would care to go to the

2

Gare de Lyons at eight in the morning, at this time of year?—except those catching the train."

He had said this in French. I retorted in French too.

"If I were you I would not be so sure no friends of yours will turn out to wish you *bon voyage.*"

"You could not, dear lady, be there as early as that," said Enoch Arnold Bennett, with bravado.

As it was I had contemplated seeing him off. I immediately made up my mind to do so.

Three days later the train to Italy was formed when I arrived at the station. On its magnificent engine blocks of ice were glittering like diamonds, for the electric light was reflected in them. People were moving on the platform in the cold and artificial light. I did not see the man I was looking for. . . . I did not care to try to find him. He was sure to see me in time. If he did not see me I would not mind; I would go back home, after his train had left, and say nothing to anybody about my morning's failure. But Mr. Arnold Bennett was not a man to miss his train. He was not a man to rush at the last minute, to leave things to chance. I now could see him advancing, wearing a thick coat, a cap and thick gloves. He carried newspapers under his arm, and he came towards me smiling, as a Frenchman would have done.

3

He said, "You have come, and in good time. I would never have believed it possible."

He did not hide his joy. It did not strike him he was being somewhat tactless in showing his surprise at my being in time. I said, "Your train does not leave for a few minutes yet."

"No, it does not. I can't get over the fact that you managed to come."

He was so struck that he neglected to thank me.

Just before his train left he said calmly, "I shall write to you from San Remo."

He did. I answered his letters. He kept on writing to me. He came back to Paris in April, and we were married there on July 4th, 1907, American Independence Day.

He told me from the very start about himself and his family. Just a few facts. That he did not care to marry young. Girls in his part of the world, the Midlands, were wondering why he did not marry. Some of his friends in London were surprised he had stayed a bachelor so long, while others wished for his own sake that he would remain one all his life. He was to please no one in such a matter but himself. He surprised a few when, a year before I met him, he told them that he was engaged to an American girl. He did not marry her. His reason to me was, "She was never in time. I could not stick it." I presume she refused to be trained that way and he came to the conclusion that his work would suffer seriously. He emphasized to me that it was a good thing for her he had given her up, for she married another man far better suited to her than he himself was.

This was candid. It showed he knew his limitations as a husband. I did not reflect upon it at the time, so convinced was I that he was out to be a perfect husband.

He told me he had lost his father seven years before and had that day made up his mind to leave England for Paris. He told me his mother was alive and that he was the eldest of a family of six. They were all married. His turn had come to make a home for himself and do away with the bother of having a home to run, orders to give—time to keep to himself for relaxation and enjoyment. He had passed the time in finding "his way out"—he was nearly forty and he had decided to marry.

"My time is free now to start a big book I have in mind. When we are married and settled it is to be written," he declared.

He also said, laughing, "I have the reputation among the members of my family and among my friends of having drawn my life, till now, on a plan—my marrying at forty will make them exclaim, 'Did he not say he would

5

marry at forty?' It is mere coincidence, though
. . . but how easy it is to make people believe
one draws one's life on a plan! One has only to
keep saying so. It is obvious that one has to
know roughly what one is after and how one
is to obtain the ultimate object. When I was
young I wanted to have money—in my part of
the world they call it 'brass'—I was kept so
short of money while a youngster. Father had
little to give us for pocket-money.

"Being the eldest son I was selected by him
to succeed him in his profession as a solicitor,
which profession he was so proud of. I became
his clerk. I went on being kept by my family,
working for Father and receiving no salary. I
was not to accept this sort of thing for long. My
ambition was to make good for myself. It had
become hopeless to expect Father would give
me a salary, for he was either not making enough
money or, more probably, he would not understand me, his son, asking him for a fixed salary,
such as he would have had to give to an outside
clerk. I made up my mind to ask him for a
salary, and I did. What I had thought, happened. He was not only surprised, he was
shocked. I told him, 'Father, if on such and
such a date you do not agree to what I have
asked, I will leave your office to be a clerk to
somebody else.'

"Father thought I did not mean it. He did not know me either, for he was entirely taken by surprise when, on the date I had fixed for him to decide about my lot, I said to him, 'Father, I am leaving you in a month's time. I have a job in London as a clerk at £1 5s. a week.'

"Father was annoyed, but, as I had said, I left him for London."

Yes, my husband told me so.

He added, "I have pretty well succeeded up till now. I will succeed in the full meaning of the term."

He has done so.

What he did not tell me at the time was, that he soon found kind friends in London. Friends who treated him as a beloved younger brother. They were artists, Mr. and Mrs. Frederick Marriott. A childless couple, most charming and true. They are still alive and have had the great sorrow to see him departing from this world too soon, full of energy, keen on his work, keen on painting, music, keener on life than ever—for he had never ceased to be intoxicated with women, femininity, and the power money gave.

He drew from vivid thoughts, from all manifestation of life, his inspiration. Morbid thoughts did not inspire him, they depressed him. His

7

mind did not dwell on the uncanny question of
the spirit never dying. Yet he has written a
wonderful book dealing with the soul of a dying
man leaving his body and analysing itself—that
book, called *The Glimpse*, was a miracle he had
settled to accomplish. It is remarkable but cannot be called poetical.

Religion had no inspiring effect on Arnold
Bennett. Though saturated in his youth with
the beautiful religion of Christ, his intellect
refused to be impressed with it. His heart
(though he was kind-hearted) rejected system-
atically all trace of religious impulse—yet at
heart he was a Christian. When he ever gave
me a chance to imagine he was fighting with
himself not to appear a Christian, I would
immediately say to him, "Don't pretend to
yourself, my dear, at heart you are more of a
Christian than many who pose as such."

He would laugh.

I have often thought that his unreligious
attitude was a garment to protect himself from
being accused of being sentimental—for religion teaches not only to be kind at heart but
to show our feelings, to express them, to talk
about eternal peace, eternal felicity, to idealize
everything for the glory of God and the joy of
man.

Arnold Bennett was not sentimental, yet he

fit the ways of the clever, interesting young clerk, busy all day and eager to work at night, so as to increase his chances in life. Like her husband and their friends, she loved young "Arnold".

Material peace and comfort he had cheaply. He knew the value of money and had full value for it there. With the fire of ambition burning in him, with hard work, patience, and perseverance, his work brought him money, the best encouragement for a young man like him. It would have been easier for him to lose his spare time in charming his friends, but as a youth he spent more time in working than in playing, when he did not work for his employer at twenty-five shillings a week.

He had determination. He was out to succeed. He did succeed.

In spite of boasting to me that he did not draw out his life to a plan, from what I have been told about the development of his career before I met him, and from what I have witnessed of his life and career ever since, it has proved to himself and to his friends that the "foreseeing" man lived his life according to plans, with the help of circumstances and hard work.

He wrote alternately for money or pleasure —always conscientiously. He candidly expressed his intense pleasure at the high prices he could get for his work. He did rather love to boast about it and to exaggerate somewhat the amount of money he was making. He juggled with prices, as a clown with golden eggs, knowing that if one publisher did not accept his price another would.

Young Enoch Arnold Bennett, born at Hanley, Staffordshire, May 27th, 1867, built up a wonderful literary career for the man Arnold Bennett—one of the greatest writers of his time.

In my heart the man and the artist have lived ever since I met him. In my heart he still is.

I

Do we think of the baby in his cradle when we bury one who has grown up? We rarely do. We can only trace in our memory events of the life of our departed ones from the day we knew them. A mother alone can remember what her baby in his cradle was like. She recollects exasperating fits of crying, which in after years she recognized as obstinacy in the baby that grew into the obstinate boy. She remembers traits of independence, cocksureness, and hidden tenderness in the youngster . . . and the mysterious, distant, teasing ways of the young man . . . later in life, the protecting affection of the man who is to her still a child needing protection. And, still later, the son following his art amongst his contemporaries. She sees in him the man sharing his life with a wife who takes care of him as she took care of him as long as he did not, like a bird, fly away from his home.

My husband's mother was buried many years before him. She was spared the tragedy of losing her eldest, beloved son; but she had missed witnessing the tribute paid to him, her baby born sixty-three years ago in modest surroundings, and dying in luxury. Proud of him she was, prouder of him she would have been if she had lived.

She was small and slim, and held herself straight and proudly. She had a clear complexion. She had no sense of humour, but she had a great sense of her duties and responsibilities. She was a devoted wife. She would work hard in the day time, and till late at night, trimming bonnets, in order to help her husband to fulfil his ambitions, which had become her own. Both had a firm, settled determination to give their children a good education and a strong moral background, derived from religion and artistic fulfilments.

The Bennett family were considered unusual and exceptional among their circle of friends. The head of the house was determined, almost hard. I am told he was a silent man. His remarks were taken as absolute orders, his orders were laws and were followed conscientiously by his dependants. Determination, supplying tradition, created the Enoch Bennett family's own tradition. The motto should have been, "Stick to it to get there." The father "got there." He wanted to become a lawyer. Late in life he did so. I do not know if he was grateful to his wife for her helpfulness with the money she earned, but I am inclined to think he took it as a matter of course.

The Victorian era saw many autocratic husbands—husbands like cockerels, feeling entirely superior through the mere fact that they were of the male sex. They had been brought up to look at themselves as being superior to girls. Mothers and sisters played up to them. Girls admired their superiority, and wives submitted amorously, dutifully or negatively to their protective, autocratic husbands. They commanded respect, to the extent of frightening one to death. If they were honest, great workers, they inspired and developed the same qualities in their children. Unless wealth was to spoil some of their offspring, inclined by nature to slack, to dream or go where fancy took them, their father's example would turn a born poet or an artist into a matter-of-fact man, pooh-poohing his own dream, in order to make good financially at whatever line life should direct him.

The middle class of the Victorian era in the Midlands was rigid, matter-of-fact, unpoetical, undemonstrative and almost ashamed of its rare fits of sentimentality. It was also secretly proud of its well-hidden kindness of heart, which could be so soft at times as to go out of its way to display indiscriminate kindness and self-denial.

Enoch Bennett, my husband's father, was extremely proud of Arnold. He did not express his admiration. On the contrary, he hid it, but

his friends were aware of it. He did not encourage his son by recognizing his merits. His
practice was to make him work by giving him
the impression that "he could do better." The
day arrived when Arnold, his eldest son, came
to the conclusion that he was "doing pretty
well"—for his twenty-one years. In order to do
better, he made up his mind to go elsewhere,
where his merits would be recognized, his
efforts encouraged and his talents find scope for
development.

In London he found appreciation, and admiration from the Londoners. He polished his
manners somewhat, changed his habits and
took care not to fall in love. He had made up
his mind to succeed first as a clerk, then as a
journalist, then as a novelist and finally as a
dramatist.

As a journalist he ended by editing a magazine, *Woman*. Free himself, as a bachelor, he
was ready when about thirty to accept the
responsibility of head of the family, and induced
his father and mother to settle with him at
Trinity Hall, Hotcliffe—not far from London
—for his father's sake. By doctor's orders his
father had to live in the country in order to
recuperate from a nervous breakdown. My
husband's second brother took his father's
business over, to free him from worry. Mr.

Enoch Bennett, the autocratic father and husband, was to the end of his life under his eldest son's roof. When he died, Arnold, his son, was about thirty-three. His two brothers and two of his sisters were married. The third sister was not.

Arnold had, the day his father died, three things in hand to settle. To bury his father, to marry his sister and to induce his mother to return to her native town, Burslem, to establish herself there for good.

His father's last breath had hardly left his body when his son, such a horror he had of corpses, ordered that it should be put immediately into a coffin and taken out of his bedroom to the greenhouse. His son had no reverence for his father's body, any more than he ever had any reverence for any corpse. He always hated illness, and he had no use for what was useless. He wanted others to think as he did in these matters and set the example by acting according to his own idea, regardless of hurting other people's feelings. He was true to himself and he followed his impulse.

His father buried, he decided to sell his home and live abroad—France had tempted him for years. However, he did not consider himself free to go until his sister should be settled in life. She was very much admired and her brother

wished her to marry one of her three principal
admirers. He made up his mind not to break
up his home before his sister should be at least
engaged. At the week-ends they had been in
the habit of having friends to stay. He asked,
in turn, his sister's three admirers. In turn he
told each of them, "No good coming again if
you don't make up your mind about marrying
my sister before you leave"—I imagine the
young man most embarrassed by such a settle-
ment. I imagine him saying, "One does not
make up one's mind in such matters as quickly
as that!"—and thinking, "Does she love me, or
is she in love with X or Y, rather than with
me?"

Arnold's tactics worked beautifully, for before
many weeks were over his sister was engaged.

Then his mother ("The Mater," as she was
always called) was taken to her native town—
happy to be back there, for she felt her son was
a great man and that she could always rely on
him.

"Mater," he had said to her, "now that you
have no husband and will be living alone, to
cheer you up I will write to you every day."

He did so, every day for thirteen years; that
is to say, till the day his mother died.

She was a great sufferer from sciatica and
rheumatism. Her letters (for she wrote very

often) were full of herself and her sufferings—full of her servant's doings—of her only sister calling on her—of her sister's doings.

She was begged not to save on doctors and chemists . . . even on her dress and bonnets . . . she was begged not to worry, not even when being teased by her humorous son.

"My mother has no sense of humour," he frequently said to me.

I had the opportunity of seeing this for myself, that is why I have referred to it before.

His mother settled in Burslem and was satisfied to be on her own. Arnold, her son, made for Paris. He was at the time earning a pretty good income from journalism chiefly, but he meant to drop part of his journalistic work to devote himself to writing novels. He had published books which gave his literary agent such great confidence in his future that he offered to advance Arnold money for years to come, so as to relieve him from devoting too much time to writing articles or pot-boilers.

So it was that he sailed to the land whose culture was so charming to him. He was not satisfied by reading French writers. He had to bathe himself in the atmosphere of Paris . . . its civilization, its intellectualities, its charm, its frivolity. He had to see for himself what a Frenchman really was like, what French girls really were. He had real freedom to study another race which appealed so persistently to his intellect.

Sure of himself he was, but not even in Paris did he mean to find his way about alone. He made sure someone should welcome his arrival there at least. It must not be anyone he might have met in England . . . it was not a compatriot he sought, nor was it to be a nonentity. It had to be a French literary man.

His friend, H. G. Wells, knew of one, the very man—the man who was translating his works into French, that is to say Henry D. Davray. It was easy for H. G. Wells to write to Henry Davray to welcome his literary colleague and great friend, and to ask him to look after him, to introduce him to the right people, etc.

He did it. So it was that the future conqueror of a first rank in English literature was from the very start in good hands.

They met for the first time at Moret-sur-Loing, near Paris, where Henry Davray had a house. Both of them wondering what the other was like, Arnold in his train to Moret and Henry on the station platform waiting for him.

It was obviously easier for Davray to spot Arnold than it was for Arnold to recognize Davray, a Frenchman amongst others.

I was told both men were delighted with the

other. Before they had reached M. Davray's house, friendship was established between them.

Arnold confided to Henry Davray his wish to be introduced to French people, for he had not left England in order to meet his compatriots, either old acquaintances or new. He wanted to know Paris—customs, habits and inhabitants.

Through Henry Davray, Arnold Bennett met interesting people. In the literary world he met, amongst others, Marcel Schwob, married to a clever actress, Marguerite Moreno—at that time a member of the *Comédie française*. She was very intelligent. She and her husband were struck with Arnold's intelligence and they soon became friends.

He met an even more interesting man, Emile Martin, a Parisian dilettante, whose ideas, tact, habits, outlook appealed to Arnold extremely. He was a bachelor. He was wealthy. He understood life. He worshipped artists and he helped them. He knew England and loved her. He spoke English, but preferred speaking French, and Arnold had the benefit of it.

This new-found friend was devoted to Arnold. He made him join his club. He took him with him to theatres, concerts, restaurants. He taught him what Paris was like. He gave him the benefit of necessary knowledge of French character and customs, so as to help Arnold

Bennett not to make serious *faux pas*. He helped
him to draw its essence from the life.

Arnold soon organized a life for himself, in
Paris. He took a small flat, 4 rue de Calais, and
furnished it.

Meanwhile, he saw the historical Fontainebleau Palace. He fell in love with the furniture
of Napoleon's period—he had to have that style
for his home. He hunted round for bargains,
with tips given to him by his devoted friend,
Henry Davray. Napoleonic furniture inspired
him; I do not mean Napoleon did, but certainly
Napoleon's love of pageantry, his tenacity,
perseverance, his success, did encourage the
worker in him; the man afraid of splendour,
sumptuousness and power, yet striving to get
them all.

To save time, money, bother, Arnold—
though he had a home of his own—used to take
his meals at restaurants. He regularly went for
his lunch to an *Établissement Duval*, in Mont-
martre. He kept his English habit of lunching
at one o'clock, contrary to the French custom.
He always had the same menu for lunch. He
always sat at the same table, kept for him by
the same waitress, who soon became his most
devoted admirer.

His dinner he took anywhere but at Duval's,
and he contrived never to have his evening meal

alone. Being alone the whole morning, alone while taking a rest after his lunch, alone for tea, at least as a rule, he had to have company at night—and he got it.

It was not long before he was popular with many. It was not long before he acquired the habit of going to theatres. I do not know if it took him long before he could speak French, but I remember him telling me, "I could read French very easily when I first went to Paris, but I could not understand what was said around me, any more than I could make myself understood."

Apparently he picked up French pretty well, for after a time he knew it well enough to address an aged lady, who had asked him to her box at the Opera, in the second person singular—which in French is used only to members of one's own family or intimate friends.

"*Tu trouves?*" he asked her, while he meant, "Do you think so?"

This sort of slip amused French people greatly.

Arnold, being in the habit of addressing his pals in this familiar way, made the usual mistake English people make, that is to "*tutoyer*" somebody when they do not mean to. Arnold loved to "*tutoyer*" his friends. He loved to hear them using slang. He was keen to learn slang. How funny he was when using his French slang! I am inclined to think his Parisian friends played tricks on him, for I have heard him using the most extraordinary expressions both in proper French and in slang—but it was a treat to hear him using such, for his delightful English accent transposed the words into ideas.

Arnold was not altogether satisfied with Paris for long. Paris, like a cancer, was undermining his energy, was robbing too much of his time. He found a place to retire to every week— again through Henry Davray. He became a boarder, then a tenant, of a modest, pensioned railway servant and his wife. They fell to his charm and persuasion, to his marvellous way of handling people when he had set his mind to do so. They became devoted to him. For a mere song he obtained a flat, breakfast and service. For a few francs he had, twice a day in an inn close by, delicious meals. With good tips, the servants were at his command and for a chat or a smile the landlady offered him the very best food she could offer—though she never forgot to present her bill. The English customer never argued about prices. He knew what he got for his money, and he was aware he was paying no more than anybody else.

The charming village where he found such a

retreat is called Les Sablons. It is near Moret-sur-Loing, close to the Forest of Fontainebleau. In this village Henry Davray had taken refuge too, to recover from a serious illness. Arnold Bennett had the benefit of his company. He was spoilt by Madame Davray herself, a born nurse, a devoted soul and a fine housekeeper; particular about herself and her house. Arnold with a word would praise her qualities and in so doing increased her devotion to him and to his friend Henry. Arnold used to call Henry *"Mon coco,"* and his wife, *"Gaby."* Their kindness to him had no limit. They were mutually happy and flattered by knowing each other.

I came on the scene later. Arnold had been living in France for nearly seven years then. It was a mutual friend who was the cause of our meeting.

I remember him telling me, when Arnold and I were married, "I knew that Bennett was struck by you when he first saw you, but I did not know he meant to marry you! I am glad for your sake, though he is rather difficult to please . . . so very exacting . . . so autocratic . . . a sort of tyrant."

"Yes, he is all you say—as a matter of fact, Monsieur Emile Martin's mother called him, in front of me, *'le bon tyran,'* and other *qualificatifs*, to imply he was fussy, difficult. Artists are rather

25

difficult to live with, but we seem to get on very well!"

My friend could not get over the fact that I had married an Englishman, I, so thoroughly French, so independent, so eager to follow a dramatic career. He did not know me. He did not guess I was craving to devote myself to an intelligent man who loved and valued me. Marriage gives scope for endless devotion. I entered into marriage with all my heart, seeing in my husband a man, a baby, a protector, to love, to help, to cheer, till death would part us. Alas! circumstances have not allowed me to spend the last few years of his life with him, but my mind, my heart have been with him ever since we married—that is to say, since the 4th July, 1907. Man could not separate the essence of us, which God had joined. Death leaves me his widow and I am proud to be his widow, as I was proud to be his wife. But how sad I feel that with comfort and care he might have lived much longer. He knew how to look after himself; that is, he did see doctors when necessary and followed their advice conscientiously—but he was not master of circumstances which overwhelmed him, wearied him. His responsibilities were great all his life, but they were greater towards the end of it. Work and worry were the two microbes which were eating up his tremendous energy and his good constitution!

He was a highly strung man and consequently suffered all through his life from nervous headaches and many nervous diseases, but, I repeat, his vitality was great. Kindness and tenderness given to him with discrimination did help him. He could not bear scenes and quarrels. They worried him, but he had to put up with them, and he did it at the expense of his health.

Worries, responsibilities, social duties, nothing stopped him for long from writing so many words a day. He had hardly finished a book when he started another one. If the strain of a book just finished had been too great, he would, as relaxation, write another book which he classed as "fantasia"—or he would write a play. He even tried himself in poetry and film work. His faith in himself was unlimited, yet he was not so very sure of himself. He had the anxiety which makes any artist feel he might have done even better, together with not being certain of being pleased himself with the work just achieved. To be in doubt about one's own work is a torment many artists are carrying with them. They do not always confess such anxiety. Their own opinion about their work is very versatile. One day they exult with the joy of "having got it"—the following day they seem to be most miserable, almost ashamed of the same work. Artists are never satisfied.

Those who really knew Arnold Bennett were aware that behind the cocksureness he was never quite satisfied with himself. I have never heard him boasting about his work or his success. I only saw him responding to the praise he got, discriminating, however, between the sincere and the insincere, in order not to be intoxicated with what might be exaggeration. He wished the candid opinion of his closest friends about his work and in his private life. He would say, "I have such and such an idea for a novel, what do you think of it? I know such and such a girl, I want to marry her. What do you think of it?"

He asked the opinion of his friend, Emile Martin, when he was thinking of asking me to marry him. He was not sure of his own judgment about me. He was on the way to being in love but he was not to fall hopelessly in love and marry me without making sure that I spoke good French. I was the sort he wanted as a wife, capable, economical, patient, adaptable, affectionate, devoted, constant, honest.

He himself told me that his friend's opinion of me was high, that he valued his opinion and that, together with his own conclusions about me, he had made certain that I was the wife for him.

"You are wrong," I had said, "I am so thoroughly French you will not be happy with me."

"It might be you who might not be with me!"

When this dialogue took place we were both in love with each other and we decided to marry.

At the time, in Arnold Bennett's mind, a masterpiece was growing. He was getting ready to create it. For the final planning of such a huge work he had to have perfect peace. He found it. A few days after we were married we left Paris for his home at the Sablons. Madame Lebert, the wife of the pensioned railway man, looked after us in the same way as she used to look after him while he was a bachelor. I was a complement to his surroundings, a joy to his eyes, for he loved my ways, my quietness, my voice, my way of dressing; adoring myself, my tall and slim figure, my dark eyes, my long black hair, my clear complexion, my small head with its quick, unexpected movements, with its straight nose, its thin lips with curves smoothing my big mouth. My Madonna type appealed to him, the man, physically so unlike me, at first sight.

He held himself straight. He was on the tall side, and slim, at the time I met him. He had dark eyes and a clear complexion. His nose was small with sensitive nostrils; it was pointed and its extremity was directed more to the sky than to the earth. His brown eyes were not piercing, but the flame of intelligence made them shine at times like those of a cat. He had a most unusual chin. A myriad chins in one. There was determination in the jaw. The chin revealed fantasy, mischief, materialism and sagacity; while his pointed, refined nose revealed humour, his eyes, understanding and keenness. Arnold's chin disturbed him, when revealed to him in a photograph or in a painted portrait.

A modern painter painted our portraits in oil about twelve years ago. Arnold's was done a year or so before mine. I had it hanging in our drawing-room in London, before mine was painted. When mine was done and framed, it was put in our drawing-room, waiting to be hung in Arnold's study.

My husband, who at the time rarely had lunch or tea at home, announced to me one day that he would come back for tea. I waited for him. I remember having a good tea for him, and I was looking forward to the joy of pouring out tea for him. He came and sat in a seat facing the mantelpiece. His portrait was hanging on the wall by his right side, and mine was placed on the floor against the wall on his left side. While having tea Arnold was very silent and his eyes were looking alternately at the two portraits. He remained looking in silence while drinking his tea. At the end of the half-hour he had for his tea, he looked once more at both portraits; then, fixing his eyes on his, he said, "I don't care what they say, I am a nice man!"

I had not made any remark whatever. It amused me and I laughed, but I am not sure that Arnold liked it.

I am sure, however, that he did not like his portrait. None of our women friends liked it. They would exclaim, "He is much nicer than that!"

I, personally, like that picture of him. I am proud to be the owner of it. The young artist who painted him was a great psychologist. I agree he was unkind, but he has got all Arnold's characteristics, the man as he was at fifty—the real man, with his qualities, his fundamental virtues and gifts; not his physical counterpart; not the man-about-town, dressed somewhat ostentatiously, wearing the very best make of clothes, shoes, hats, shirts, gloves, handkerchiefs, ties; but the man who wore every day a fresh carnation in his button-hole—a carnation grown by our own gardener at our country house and devotedly brought to him at week-ends by his faithful secretary or sent to him by our gardener. His button-hole decorated, his hat somewhat on one side, his stick and his heels clapping the pavement of Bond Street, Piccadilly, etc. . . . he was triumphantly marching to his club to meet his friends and have lunch with them. I had grown, by then, to know that an Englishman cannot do without his club or clubs.

II

ARNOLD BENNETT at forty was out for tranquillity and peace when we married. From the very start of our married life, as I have said before, we retired to the country. He had but little time for me, who so much wanted him to spend his spare time with me. But he was not to cease his interest in me after the intensive companionship of a banal honeymoon. He did not believe in that—it was not his way of understanding marriage. He was to carry out his plan of having friends from London to come over and spend the summer with us directly we were married. I begged him to ask his friends to postpone their visit till the following summer, but he declared it could not be done. I had the explanation of it all much later.

When the husband of the couple we were expecting heard that Arnold, his friend, had married, he wrote to him saying that, under the circumstances, he and his wife would give up the arrangements made with him for this holiday.

Arnold answered, "Nothing of the kind, my boy, I shall need you more than ever before!"

He could not do without friends round him

for long, but he loved to choose his own time for visitors. He did not think so much of the pleasure they might derive from his company as he thought of the interest, diversion and amusement it would give him to have them. His constant object was to get out of life, out of people, what could be got—toward the one end, his work. He was the medium of his work. He could but at rare intervals "let himself go"— get away from analysing himself and others. He was self-conscious in the extreme. Therefore, to hide it, he would act some sort of part and, with his intimates, play the fool or be somewhat hard and brutal, domineering, or almost submitting to cowardice. Whatever mood he was in, he always retained attention. His joining in anything meant leadership. He knew his mind. One had only to follow, for he was a born leader.

In that summer, 1907, he organized our outings. We did a lot of cycling. We would, in the afternoon, under the burning sun, cycle some distance away to have tea, or to find out a nice spot as a subject for a water-colour sketch.

Arnold's keenness for drawing and water-colour was great. Our visitors were artists . . . he was not to miss his chance of learning, and he did improve.

When we did not go out he would make a

My husband's favourite portrait of me.

drawing of me. I had to keep moveless, and I hated it. I was self-conscious and bored . . . but in order to give him pleasure I submitted. I would say, when he showed the portrait he had made of me, "Not so bad!" I would laugh. He did not smile. He would not be teased on the result of his hobby. He was serious about his efforts, like a child in the act of destroying a toy.

In the village he was a king, a sort of exiled king. Everybody saluted him. They respected him and his friends. He was thought to be very rich, as most English and American people are by the working folk and all the population of a small village. He looked terribly English in his well-cut suit, or when he turned up as a country squire. He attracted attention. People would make remarks about him on the quiet, while dogs would bark at him when, in his baggy knickerbockers, his leggings, his cap and his stick in hand, he would wander round the country alone.

Once a dog attacked him.

"I can't think why dogs should go for me," he said.

"My dear, dogs hate tramps. They take you for one!"

"They shouldn't."

But dogs would go on being surprised at his clothes, and barked, fearing for their lives, while

35

Arnold feared lest he should be bitten and sent to the Institute Pasteur, in Paris, to be inoculated against hydrophobia. He never was, though!

It did happen that dogs would run after us while we cycled (for French dogs of that period were not yet used to cycles).

"Confound the beasts!" Arnold would say.

He would at times swear, and I did as he did without realizing I was doing so. Once I fell, out of fatigue, from my machine and exclaimed, "Damn the thing!"

Arnold said, "You should not say such things. It is not done."

"Is it not? but you do it, my dear."

"It is not the same."

"I don't see the point."

"Of course you don't."

He then appealed to our visitors and they both agreed it was better for me never to use such an expression again. I found such English expressions so appealing that I often used them in my mind when out of patience. Even mental swearing has a magic effect in relieving one of irritation. It is supposed to be un-Christian and bad form to swear. As it does bring relief to one it seems that Christ himself would not have condemned even swearing. Society cannot prevent mental bad language. It is, however, wise to avoid bad habits, and swearing is one of the easiest habits to form.

The sweet English couple who spent that summer with us never swore. They were easy to get on with. They were out to please. I missed them when they had to return to London.

Autumn was drawing on and it was time for us to return to Paris, as it was arranged before we were married. But my husband had decided otherwise. He had no wish to return to Paris. His wish was to stay at Les Sablons until Christmas and take me to England for a while. We did both.

He was proud to introduce me to his brothers and sisters.

One of his sisters at first terrified me. When I first saw her I kissed her, but she was not to be kissed so impulsively, not even by her French sister-in-law whom she had so kindly accepted into the family—by letter. No. She stood straight, smiling, but on her guard, and looked severe. It paralysed me. I blushed as if I had committed a crime.

Behind her appeared her husband, all smiles too, but less stern, and obviously most reverend to the sex. He looked more human. His wife was very much like Arnold in looks. He was not unlike St. John, and, like him, he had grown a beard. He was kind and condescending.

37

The true spirit of hospitality was there no doubt from the very first, but I could not feel it for days.

I remember saying to my husband, in despair, *"Cheri, je m'ennuie!"*

My *cheri* turned pale and anxiously said, "What shall I do?"

There was apology in the tone of his voice. I comforted him, after upsetting him, and I was extremely cross with myself for my lack of self-control.

Sympathetic as my husband was, he had no patience with those who could not keep their emotions to themselves. I was, at the time, under the delusion that one could always let oneself go with one's better half—but apparently no two people can be really themselves with each other. Certainly in the Five Towns, in Arnold's time, they were not trained to have perfect confidence, even in the chosen one. A great French writer has said and written, *"Chaque anglais est une île."*

My sister-in-law was an island.

It seems to me that English people, more than any other race, have realized that the best way to avoid reaction is not to explain, not to argue, not to complain, not to discuss. In order to have as much tranquillity as possible, they have willingly sacrificed, *le laisser aller*, *la fantaisie*, candid sayings and doings. They keep their emotion inside. In so doing they do more damage to themselves than to others. They seem to like that way best. They certainly act according to habit and temperament.

Arnold was tremendously English to me, in spite of his charming ways and the superficial polish the atmosphere of Paris had given him. There was a gap between his manners acquired late in life and the cold hard way he was brought up. He was a sympathetic and good listener. He was generous by nature and also because he wanted to be. He had, hidden in his nature, a sense of justice, and he acted accordingly. His forgiveness was on the whole not difficult to obtain if you offended him. He would forgive, forget real offence from those he had a fancy for, but he could be pitiless for a mere *faux pas*. His equals paid heavily when they went too far. Their kind feelings towards him were not taken into consideration. Those needing his intellectual and material protection were easily forgiven and helped. They often gained by having shown they were capable of timid rebellion and of apologizing humbly. He delighted in the good he could do those needing help. He was rarely short of a kind word to encourage, guide and help. He never drew back from his word. When he had said, "I will

help you," he did help. If it was that he was
to read a book and criticize it, he would read
the book and tell the author candidly what he
thought of it. He had the ability to put clearly
what he meant, either in letter writing or in
speech. Short sentences. He loved full stops in
both senses. In talking especially this was the
case. His brain worked quickly, but he had not
facility of expression because of a most affecting
but regrettable stammering, which at times
threatened him with complete loss of speech.
One seldom heard him stammer when talking
French, and when it did happen in front of me
I acted as if I had not noticed it. To me he did
not stammer. It was never mentioned between
us. He never referred to his stammering to me,
but I knew he had done his very best to cure
himself entirely of such a hindrance to his
ambition. I have often thought it was a blessing
from God that he was prevented from adding
to his huge task the temptation of making
speeches, giving lectures, etc.

Once we were asked to a big dinner party at
Stoke-on-Trent Town Hall. Arnold was the
guest of honour. He was urged at the end of the
meal to make a speech. I was nervous for him.
He answered that he would not, but the gathering would not hear of it. They clapped until
Arnold rose. My heart beat. I was afraid under

the stress of emotion he would stammer. But
standing up he looked cheerful and calm. His
fountain pen, with its gold cap, was shining in
the upper pocket of his evening jacket. He
stood straight. All eyes were fixed intently on
him. He took his fountain pen out of his pocket,
and showing it to them, he said, "Ladies and
gentlemen, I don't speak, I write," and sat
down.

The impulsive man, the business man, the
comedian in him have had compensations from
this hindrance—for how affecting and useful
stammering can become and did become. His
sense of humour, his sarcasm, his prudence were
intensified by this awkward infirmity which
was his lot. I do not know to what extent he
suffered from it. I only know that he tried to
cure himself at different times in his life. At
fifty-two he followed a course of experiment on
the quiet. He was not aware that I knew of
it. He did many things on the quiet. It was
astonishing how I would be kept informed by
circumstances. My intuition helping, there was
very little I did not actually know or guess
rightly. It did happen at times that, feeling
hurt by his lack of confidence, I could not keep
his childish secrets to myself, and I would
childishly hint at them. He would say, "How
do you know? I have not told you."

While staying in London with his sister's family I heard many things about him, his ways, his character, through a friend of the family. She spoke French fluently and knew the Bennett family pretty well and Arnold particularly well.

"Everyone looks up to him, my dear. He is the great man of the family and can do no wrong! Yet when we all heard he was married we said, 'Whoever he has married, we don't give them six months before they part.' He has always been peculiar but you have changed him already. He is so very charming . . . what have you done to him? As for you, you do look thin and pale. You know while his sister was running his house, just a few years before he went to live in France, she worried greatly because he was always making remarks and was so fussy . . . he is very exacting; charming but peculiar. Well, I dare say you have found it out already!"

I had, to a certain extent, in the few months just passed alone with him at Les Sablons.

This friend of his did not disturb me a scrap, for I was delighted to hear her speak of my husband. Her admiration for him was hidden in the tone of her voice and at the back of every word she used. She described my husband's mother to me, the friends of his family who

lived at the Potteries, Arnold's two brothers, his
two elder sisters, and his "in-laws." This was
a thoughtful and kind deed. It did help me
when I was actually taken to Burslem by my
husband.

He was proud and very excited when he
introduced me to his mother. He first took off
his hat—apparently quite calm—and then his
coat, in the hall, while his mother in the sitting-
room close by also waited calmly till the maid
opened the door.

"Hello, Mater! Here she is," said her son,
pushing me into the room.

I did not kiss her; my experience with her
daughter living in London prevented me. She
kissed me. She said little. She did not smile.
She looked at me. She knew a lot about my
everyday doings. Arnold in his daily letters to
her used and abused me as a target for his filial
sentimental literature. Marguerite's dress, headaches, walks, dogs were inexhaustible daily
sources for him to draw copy from. I had had
(reading his letters) many headaches that I had
never had, so many that the Mater soon became
anxious. She wrote, "It is a pity your wife is so
delicate. After this last attack you should call a
doctor."

"Arnold, I have not been ill. What does this
mean?"

"You see, I must fill the pages, must not I?" was his answer.

What could I do but be amused?

Now the Mater saw me for the first time in the flesh, she being very small thought me very tall, taller than I really was. She thought I looked well.

She poured out tea for us. I perceived she and her son did not talk much, and certainly there was no manifestation of joy. I understood little of what they said.

Presently, when in our bedroom—her own bedroom, where an extra bed had been put for the occasion—my husband said to me, "I can tell the Mater likes you. I shall have to be on my guard."

She was proud to have us. Her maid was as proud as her mistress. She somewhat lost her head. She had never seen a Frenchwoman before. The first one happened to be the daughter of the house. It was magic and unheard of in the Potteries.

Arnold greatly enjoyed the romantic side of it. That he had married at forty, and a Frenchwoman, a Parisienne! Just like him. The rebellious young man leaving the Potteries . . . the clever man, getting on, doing better and better, and ending by doing nothing else but writing, and writing books out of his knowledge

44

of the Potteries . . . and being rich through it all! Disturbing! . . . marvellous!

Arnold was a marvel and he enjoyed being a marvel.

"Here she is," he said each time he introduced me to his relations and friends.

He occasionally would say, "Here is my wife."

I was made a fuss of, but not in an ostentatious way. The middle class of the Potteries is not to such an extent so undignifiedly brought up.

"Don't show your feelings . . . keep them inside you . . . but open your house. Be hospitable. Give the best you can get in food and drink . . . and when having guests, don't forget to make your high tea higher than ever! Pay no compliments but be more polite."

We were asked out to high tea and to dinner all the short time we stayed with the Mater.

"Shall I have you once to dinner with me before you go back?" asked the Mater of her son one day.

It was arranged we should have dinner with her next day.

Personally, I spent many hours with the Mater; while Arnold, hardly having swallowed the last mouthful of a good breakfast, would leave us. He had explained to me that he was taking notes for his next book, *The Old Wives'*

45

Tale, which was to deal with the Potteries and
local people. We saw little of him in the afternoon either.

The day we left he asked that breakfast be
served somewhat earlier.

"Why?" said the Mater. "Your train does not
leave as early as all that."

"I shall have to go out after breakfast."

"Shall you?"

The dear old lady did not speak her mind,
but her regret was that she had seen too little
of that son who had, to the last, so little time
for her. She said nothing to him about it.
Mothers bear a lot with resignation. They have
more power to give than to receive.

I remember her that morning in her sitting-
room where breakfast had been served. She
was in black as usual, looking, as always, handsome and sweet, stiff and straight. She wore her
usual expression, which was in reality a mask
behind which was hidden whatever thought
and feelings might pass through her consciousness. She had a natural expression which was
neither repellent nor attractive. It made me
feel self-conscious as well as matter-of-fact, and
I longed to go back to France where we were
to settle in Fontainebleau.

The Mater was not sure that I understood
her when she addressed me. That morning she

wanted to make sure I should understand what she had to say, to me in particular, before we departed. Arnold having left us, she asked what I thought of my visit to the district. I do not know if she understood my answer.

"We haven't seen much of him, have we? You are to have him always. I am pleased he has got you. I may die in peace now. Remember that if at any time you don't get on I shall know it is not your fault."

While saying this she had left her seat and had put her hand on my shoulder. I was moved. What a tremendous faith the old soul had in me! How she made me feel my responsibilities as a wife! . . . one to whom she, the mother, was entrusting her son, to fulfil her part as a mother to the grown-up child, difficult to understand, and from whom she feared alarming moods, lack of propriety and modesty. Proud of her son she was, believing in him, she did, but he made her suffer with his sarcasm, his great sense of humour, his outspoken opinion about religion and against religion, his candid criticism of the way he had been brought up— saturated in religion and in narrow-mindedness —his criticism of his mother's only sister, his aunt: so eager to do and say what would hurt no one though being at heart hard and un-generous. To her nephew she was a hypocrite.

Ah! how powerless the Mater was to stop her son from teasing her about her sister! How eager I was to appease the disturbance Arnold was creating in her! How he laughed when I said to the Mater one day, "Please, don't take him seriously. He is only teasing you, Mother."

This made Arnold say at another time, "A mother can't be deceived about her children. She knows them all right!"

III

A FEW months later we settled in a small house at Avon-Fontainebleau, rue Bernard Palissy. It was called Villa des Néfliers.

Mercilessly Arnold had altered the plan of the house. Walls had come down. The small bedroom made into a big one. Another was turned into a bathroom. Two reception rooms were made into a large one. No study on the ground floor. There was a poky room which was used occasionally as a dining-room (we had our meals in a kiosk in the garden which was not far from the kitchen). The kitchen was small but had a very good gas cooker. A small room on the first floor had to be used as Arnold's study. It had a view of the garden at the back of the house. It opened on to a small landing at the top of the stairs, and into our bedroom.

Arnold arranged it very well. A bookcase against one of the panels of the room, an easy-chair by the mantelpiece and the window, and against the wall, where the door of our bedroom was, Arnold's writing-desk was placed. In front of it a handsome Empire desk-chair. On the walls, pictures. On the table a few well-bound books and dictionaries in a row. In the drawer of the desk were the white sheets of paper which were specially ordered for the manuscript of the book my husband was going to start writing. The book he had had in mind for ever so long.

The time had at last come when he could start it. His surroundings were his own choice; the time of meals was chosen to suit him. The hell of creation was to torment the artist in an earthly paradise for months to come.

He was looking forward to beginning that book, as he would have looked forward to a new experiment. He had heard that an English writer, who was known to him, when writing wanted his wife to play the piano in the next room. Arnold did not wish to hear the piano played while he wrote, but he wanted to see what effect my presence in his study would have.

He said, "Suppose you bring your sewing into my study and do it while I write?"

I was happy that he had asked me such an unexpected favour.

After he had had his afternoon rest that day I joined him with my needlework.

"Sit on the easy-chair by the mantelpiece."

I sat comfortably, placing my work-basket on another chair by me. Arnold at his desk started writing.

I could hear his pen running over the sheet

of paper. I could almost hear him breathing. It made me conscious of my own breathing and I feared it might disturb him, so I breathed carefully. Then my needle would rattle on the thimble and make a noise. I thought the noise would disturb the lover-writer of mine.

He turned his head, looked in my direction but said nothing. He resumed his pen and I my needlework.

The thread I was using came to an end and I took a reel for more, but the reel fell on the floor! Arnold looked at me. I was aware that I had disturbed him.

After a while I wanted to cough. I controlled myself. Then by an unfortunate accident my thimble fell down. Arnold looked at me again.

I was paralysed by the desire not to disturb him. When the first experience was up Arnold said, "Thank you for having sat here."

I breathed freely.

Next day we started again. Similar accidents happened. A reel of thread fell on the polished floor. I apologised. Arnold did not look round. He murmured, "I can't expect you to become a mouse."

I believe a mouse would have disturbed him.

I was far from being a mouse, and so I was dismissed from my husband's study while he was writing.

Before starting that important work Arnold had a surprise for me. A surprise I valued tremendously. Knowing I admired his handwriting, to the extent of picking up from the waste-paper basket the manuscript of articles just published, even of a book just published, knowing that I was interested in his hobby of classic calligraphy, he had decided to write his most vital work, *The Old Wives' Tale*, in printed characters, so that I might have it. (I am proud to say that I am responsible for Arnold keeping the manuscripts of all his works ever since.)

I could scarcely believe it possible. But what he had said he would do he did. He had the tremendous patience, energy and capacity to carry it through the whole book, which is very long, nearly seven hundred pages.

He would say, at times, "I wish to the deuce I had never started doing it that way. It has to be done, hard as it is!"

He stuck to it. A huge task only possible to a man of determination. He succeeded in both printed characters and the characters of the book. The double creation is perfect and has been proclaimed to be so.

The book took him exactly eight months to write.

What an achievement and what a success! It

was the book of the year. The book which classed him as a master. The book which is still mentioned as his best book. The success of that book allowed him to fulfil his desires in every direction in which his ambitious soul stirred him.

He was afraid his book, "the book," on which all his future depended, would, like all the others he had written up till then, either never be seen by important critics or would not be understood at all by the public at large.

Critics proved to Arnold that they did their work conscientiously. The public took notice of what the critics wrote. His editor had made a success. Arnold's friends were proud of him. He thought it fair that his genius should be recognized at last.

It was only when Arnold's reputation was firmly established that we returned to London, for a while, to see for ourselves the extent of his popularity. Truly that writer, who had worked so conscientiously at this work he had settled to do, writing chiefly for art's sake, deserved to be rewarded for his efforts. "Having got there," he meant to remain there at all costs.

"We shall be very wealthy," he used to say at times.

Soon after the success of *The Old Wives' Tale* he said to me, "We shall be very rich. I will see to it. You may rely on me, my child!"

It used to alarm me. I had no wish to be extremely wealthy. I knew it meant perpetual hard work for my husband. I knew it meant seeing less and less of him.

The literary success of *The Old Wives' Tale* in England made a young American publisher, George Doran, determine to secure the right to publish the book over there. He wrote to Arnold that he was coming to Paris and wanted to see him. Arnold guessed he was after his book.

He told me, "We must ask the fellow here for dinner, and impress him with a really good dinner!"

"It is a big order, my dear. With only my inexperienced maid and my own efforts it cannot be done."

"Of course it can."

"I should have thought the best way would be to ask him to a restaurant."

"No, he will prefer to be treated as a member of the family. I know what publishers are; but I repeat it has to be a first-class dinner."

The day that prince came to dine we had accepted an invitation to a reception, starting at 11 p.m.—a soirée. I reminded my husband of it.

"I know, we shall take him with us, that's all," he said.

54

Evidently Arnold knew how to treat publishers!

"We must impress the fellow," he repeated. "It means business."

In his mind he had his plan about business. In my mind was the planning of a menu, composed of dishes made by my seventeen-year-old maid, myself and unknown hands employed by a reputed firm of caterers.

Doubting the ultimate success of our enterprise, I suggested again that we should take our important guest to a restaurant first, then bring him back to our house for coffee.

"Nothing of the kind," said Arnold. "Besides being cheaper, it will be much nicer. You manage it all. I know it will be a success. I shall look after the wines and cigars."

We asked him to dine with us two in our modest home: a small furnished house, rue de Grenelle, Paris, we had rented for the winter months.

It was very cold the evening he came. It was difficult to make the place warm. I had a good fire in the dining-room and in the sitting-room. Both rooms were small. One was on the ground floor—the dining-room—the other on the first, and only, floor.

There was no electric light in the house, only gas in the kitchen. We had paraffin lamps. I was in the habit of doing the lamps myself, not troubling the maid with such a simple but important task.

Arnold would say, "Lamps are delicate things. They have to be done with care. No servant can do it properly."

He seemed to know a lot about lamps, about everything in the house. His knowledge of housekeeping was uncanny, redoubtable. It interested him. He had been interested in both the theoretical and practical side of it for years. Theoretically, when he was in his thirties, by editing a magazine (*Woman*) of his own, and by writing articles for it that the most well-informed woman could not have written better. He was aware of it. To attract and mystify his readers, he would sign his articles with women's names. Practically, because he was a bachelor until he was forty, and had a home of his own.

Arnold knew what a well-looked-after lamp was like. He did not mind lighting one when the occasion arose. He would at times fidget with lamps. He loved lamps. He had had them all his youth, then again at Hotcliffe, and at Les Sablons in France. He was rather enjoying the primitive home of the rue de Grenelle, where he was, that evening, to entertain George Doran, his future American publisher, so as to make him pay a fair price for the books already written and to be written. Then he would become rich enough in years to come to replace paraffin lamps, poky furnished houses and rooms in second-class inns or hotels by permanent comfort and luxury, so necessary to his future happiness.

His chance had come. He was to see to it.

"Trust me, my child."

How often he said it, when alarmed at his coolness I was afraid he might break his wings. I did trust him, yes, but my mind being infected by the habit of driving for security, I was doubtful what ultimate happiness great wealth would bring us.

With *The Old Wives' Tale* and Mr. George Doran riches entered our home and stayed there for good.

Arnold was aware of it. Not only was he all expectation waiting for the newcomer that cold winter night, but he was excited, nervous— doing all he could not to let himself go, contrary to his habit, not expressing his feelings with gestures or words.

As for me I had spared no money or trouble. I was anxious that the evening should be a success. I begged the maid to be careful when waiting at table, to wear her best apron, to look nice, to be sure to open the front door directly she heard a knock. She in her kitchen, and we upstairs in our sitting-room. . . . She was very likely thinking, "What a fuss about a foreign visitor!"

I was saying to Arnold, "You do look perfect in your evening clothes."

He answered, "Your dress might be envied by any actress from the *Comédie française!*"

This because it was not unlike *le grand siècle*, made with white lace and pompadour ribbons. It was indeed a beautiful dress, my best. Secretly we were proud of one another for being what we were, looking wealthy and certainly able to make the best of our possessions.

We waited, convinced that everything was as perfect as possible under the circumstances. Even our poky, romantic house was most fascinating, and would charm the most prosaic of American publishers!

Our publisher gave a knock at the door. Arnold immediately and most amiably descended a few steps of the narrow stairs to welcome him. A gas jet lighted the stairs from the tiny hall. The sitting-room lamp and candles on the mantelpiece were giving a bright light. The room was very warm and a big fire enhanced the light there.

"How nice it is here!" exclaimed our visitor. "Most romantic!"

His smiling, round face expressed surprise

and delight. It was something new to him. The author of *The Old Wives' Tale* could but be living in such a place . . . and with it all he was a man of the world, dressed as such, charming in the extreme and making one feel at home.

George Doran was charmed from the very minute he met "Arnold Bennett." He was himself a charming guest, with an amiable, appealing way. We all of us felt at ease from the beginning. It was delightful.

I must confess I understood little of what he said. His American accent made his English less intelligible to me than English spoken by English people. It was not important to me whether I understood him or not. My part, even had I understood him perfectly, was to let Arnold lead the conversation to his liking with regard to business. My part was essentially to play the hostess as well as was in my power.

"Dinner is ready," the maid told us, by ringing a tiny bell.

Arnold turned the wick of the lamp down and I led the men downstairs.

"How perfectly lovely this home is!" said Mr. Doran.

I thought, "Were he on the fat side I doubt these stairs would not be wide enough!"

When we entered the small dining-room our guest exclaimed again, "How charming! You

59

could not have pleased me more than by asking me to your haven . . . perfectly lovely!"

He found everything lovely. He left half of his food on his plate, did not drink good Burgundy served to him, but liked champagne, for he drank it. He made no remark either on the food or the wine. I wondered if, like spirits, he had no use for material nourishment.

Time for coffee and liqueurs had come.

I was in the habit of making the coffee myself in the dining-room, in a Russian coffee machine. It had a spirit lamp, a pot made in two parts; one for the water, the other for the coffee. The two pots were screwed together by a straight handle. The pot containing the water was to be placed on the flame of the spirit lamp, and when it boiled the double pot had to be turned upside-down so as to allow the water to run through the coffee. To turn the pot on the wrong side was fatal. The process was extremely simple, yet it meant being careful.

That evening, as usual, the machine had been put on a tray with matches, cups, sugar and milk. It was placed in front of me, after the table had been cleared of plates, glasses, etc., on the immaculate table-cloth.

Arnold said, "Marguerite, suppose you go upstairs to see after the room."

I understood business was to be discussed.

"All right," I said, "just let me make the coffee first."

"I can look after it," said Arnold, "it will not be the first time."

He had forgotten it was.

"All right," I said. "But be sure to turn it on the right side . . . that way . . . you see?"

"Yes, yes. Oh, these wives will be wifely! They think we can't do such simple things!"

I laughed, but I was not so certain as all that that my husband, who knew so well how to give orders to make others carry them out, was able to do a thing as simple as this.

I left the two men discussing business and went upstairs. A strange smell struck me half-way up. I soon made out it was the smell of smoke from paraffin.

It was!

When I opened the sitting-room door I was blinded by a thick cloud of pestilential smoke. My instinct was to shut the door again. I had on my best dress, my face was clean. My hair must be saved from this black, greasy destroyer of that which was perfect. But there was also no time to lose. I must stop the cause of such a disaster. I rushed into our bedroom close by, and clothed in an overall, old gloves, a large handkerchief on my head as a bonnet, I went

into the chamber of mischief again. I drew the
large curtains, opened the window wide and
turned down and blew out the lamp. I guessed
that Arnold, in his excitement, had turned the
wick up instead of down.

The intense cold of the air entering the room
soon dissipated the thick cloud. A deep coat of
soot covered everything in the room. I called
the maid to my aid.

"Oh, madam! . . . and you wearing your
best dress! Will you not take it off?"

"We have not time, Christine. Let us hurry.
Ces messieurs will want to come up soon. Did
you give them liqueurs and cigars?"

"Yes, madam."

I knew I should have taken my dress off, but
it meant undoing dozens of hooks fixed at the
back, hooks that had taken Arnold and me
ever so long to fasten, and hooks which would
take Christine and me endless time to refasten,
and would so irritate me! I could not bear to
take my dress off.

"Let us hurry," I said to Christine.

She shook the rugs and cushions through the
window. I dusted the mantelpiece, etc. I made
up the fire, put new wood on it.

Christine said, "I had no time to look after
that fire, madam, as I meant to. I wish I had
found time. Then this accident would not have

occurred and madam would not have had to wash again."

I looked in the looking-glass on the mantel-piece and saw, popping out of the handkerchief, dark eyes and a dark pointed nose, darker with the soot where I had unconsciously placed my dirty gloves.

I laughed, left Christine to finish cleaning the room and rushed into my bedroom again. The nasty smell had penetrated my clothes and I no longer felt neat and elegant. I willingly endured for a few minutes the intense cold in front of my bedroom window so as to get rid of the unpleasant smell. Then I went downstairs with Christine.

I opened the dining-room door to find my husband in front of a huge black mark on the white table-cloth. All the contents of the coffee-pot were on the table, making a frightful mess.

"I am glad you have come," said Arnold calmly. His expression was appealing. It apologised for his clumsiness.

The two men looked pathetic in front of this mess which separated them as an unexpected sea separates two continents. There was nothing to be said. I called Christine, ordered her to fix the coffee machine again and bring it up to the sitting-room, with what was needed, including the liqueurs.

63

Half-way up Arnold said, "Strange smell."

I thought, "You are responsible for everything," but I said nothing.

Entering the sitting-room Arnold said, "By jove, it is cold here!"

I thought, "Whose fault is it?" I said nothing.

Arnold walked straight to the thermometer (it was one of his fads) and said, "There is only so many degrees in this room. Strange with such a big fire! What has happened?"

I had to confess that the window had to be left open because the lamp had been turned too high and had smoked all the time we were having dinner.

"You should be more careful is all I have to say," said Arnold.

I did not care to discuss it.

He never admitted that he had turned the wick of the lamp himself. It was strange but my dear husband would not admit himself in the wrong, not even in a mere trifle. One had to guess that in his heart he did acknowledge when he had been in the wrong.

Indeed, that reception for Mr. George Doran, which we had wanted to be perfect, was spoilt by two appalling, humiliating accidents. But this did not prevent Mr. Doran from being amiable all the time, and declaring, "It was all so lovely." He was the embodiment of a perfect guest.

When he spoke of leaving us for his hotel, Arnold said, "But we are taking you with us to a most Parisian reception and to a beautiful hostess. You can't leave us like that."

"I must. I have had a full day and to-morrow I am to meet people on business. It would be lovely to accept but I must go back to my hotel."

"Marguerite, make him come," said Arnold in French.

A few minutes later we were in the rue de Grenelle, looking for a four-wheeler (a *fiacre*) for the three of us.

The evening was a unique affair for George Doran. He was lost in admiration before our hostess. Perhaps love at first sight. He declared he had never seen anything like it before, nor a better-dressed woman. I expect he thought he had conquered Paris, for at last he knew some of its most famous inhabitants in the artistic and political world.

Arnold in an evening had conquered George Doran and knew him pretty well. George Doran had induced him to go to America. Both knew what they were after. Both were at the beginning of the financial success of their efforts. They realized at once that a close collaboration would be to the advantage of both, and they have backed one another up all through Arnold's life.

Doran Publishers published all Arnold's work in America. Arnold pointed out to George the work of writers worth publishing, with amazing success ultimately. Being a critic he knew what he was saying. In that direction, a mere suggestion from Arnold Bennett was enough to induce Doran to publish a writer.

It was through Arnold that Mrs. Asquith (Margot), now Lady Oxford and Asquith, and Mr. George Doran met, and consequently a huge amount was paid by him to Lady Oxford for the publication of her Memoirs, which were a great success. A few years before, again through my husband, the works of Mr. Frank Swinnerton and of Hugh Walpole were published by Doran. In recent years I can point out Miss Sheila Kaye-Smith, Rebecca West, Pauline Smith and numerous others, known and unknown to me.

To be under the protection of Arnold Bennett meant ultimate success. He had the gift of constructive criticism for those he believed could write; while to those who wanted to write, but who, to his mind, had no gift, he would say, "Keep trying, but don't be disappointed if you don't succeed." When the case was hopeless he would say, "It is a hard job, but it is not the only job in the world."

Years afterwards he used to say to me at times, "I don't know what made me write. I would much rather be in business. Don't be surprised if, one day, I give the 'job' up."

As if he ever could! He loved his "job." It suited his personality.

IV

MR. DORAN said, "You come to New York, Mr. Bennett, and I will see what I can do for you. The great thing is for you to show yourself!"

"Yes, I see that," Arnold would say. "But I don't know that I am keen about showing myself. I hate it really . . . and what about the trouble of finding my way about in New York and so on? I could not face it."

"I see that," George Doran, the publisher, responded to Arnold Bennett, the author. "But there is no question of your being on your own. I will see to that."

He "saw to that." In New York George Doran was Arnold Bennett's shadow and appeared to be entirely at his service. They went touring together. Arnold did not speak in public, but he was to be seen with George at meetings, gatherings and lectures.

He hated it all but enjoyed his success. It was a strenuous life for him, only made possible because he took two baths a day and was adulated by women. They swarmed round him like bees round an exotic flower suddenly sprung up for their delight. Like a helpless flower, Arnold's energy was exhausted but his interest in his vampires was great. He mercilessly declined to be absolutely swallowed up, remembering that he had a wife, his work and that he had not yet secured the first rank in English literature.

He came back with contracts signed for three books. This was the saving of us financially through the Great War, for he was able to write these books.

When Arnold came back he had, in spite of himself, broken the hearts of a few girls. A married woman, brilliant, intelligent, sensitive, had confided in him her disappointment in her marriage and her blessing in her motherhood. She found in him a sympathetic and understanding listener, a confessor in whom she had such belief that she begged him to write to her. They exchanged letters for about a year. Arnold showed her letters to me. She sent a lovely photograph of herself to him, and he asked me what he should do with it. I knew he was secretly wishing to have it about. I took the photograph and put it on the mantelpiece in his study.

"Oh! you put it there," Arnold said. That was all.

He had mine on his writing-table.

Soon after this the lady, her husband and her

boy came to England. They visited us in our English home and took photos of it.

When my husband said to her, "Here is my wife," she looked surprised and said, "But how nice she looks!"

She was refined and friendly. In the course of the day she emphasized how happy she was to discover that I spoke English so well, that I was the right companion for the genius, my husband.

Back in London she sent a kodak to me like the one she had brought with her to take views of our home and of ourselves.

She and her husband and her son returned to New York. She died soon after their visit. She left a souvenir to Arnold.

I felt the death of this extremely feminine and handsome woman, dying so young from a mysterious nervous disease. For years after this episode her photo remained where I had put it, and would have been left on the mantelpiece had we not sold the house, "Comarques."

At that time admiration from other women for my husband meant admiration for me as well. Was I not the favourite? . . . the one whose unrealized power was preventing him from becoming "loose"! For I have always seen that Arnold was fascinated by women, as well as being afraid of them. He was at home with them, especially with those of his own social class. He never praised any woman to me, only saying, "She is the right sort." He never criticized a woman to me, only saying, "I don't like her."

His judgment about men he met or knew was expressed in about the same way. "He is a nice fellow," or, "He is a rascal," or, "He is damnably clever," or, "He is the biggest conspirator who ever lived, since Napoleon died."

Yet in his heart he was less cutting about people. He had no jealousy, no bitterness, but he loved to do and say what he liked regardless of consequences. He knew how to make himself loved, and, what was more important, he knew how to retain his friends' love. His gift in this way had its drawbacks. He cursed at times the damnable influence his personality had on people. He was overwhelmed by the admiration of those who looked up to him. He found it both sweet and upsetting.

V

THE few months we spent in Paris that winter
were fully occupied. We entertained little because we did not feel rich enough nor did we
have a home organized for entertaining. We
occasionally had friends to spend the evening
with us. Arnold did not wish to have late
nights for the work had to be done. It did
not prevent us going to a few shows. Concerts
attracted my husband more than French
plays. He did not think at all highly of the
Comédie française, nor did he value French
drama much.

Almost every Sunday night we went to the
"At Home" of friends of ours, M. and Mme. X.
They were most charming. It was always a
treat to go to their gatherings. We met famous
men there, or men on the way to becoming
famous. Maurice Ravel was a regular visitor,
so was Debussy, Deodora de Severac, Paul
Valer, Valer Larbaud of the musical world,
etc., Herman Paul, André Gide, Paul Fargue
of the literary world, etc., and a future famous
French publisher called Grasset. Amongst
painters, Pierre Bonnard, Valloton, Redon,
etc. The sculptor, Rodin, was to be seen occa-

sionally. Actors, actresses and professional beauties were among this intellectual crowd.

About eleven o'clock some refreshments were served. They were put on the dining-room table and each guest helped himself, except to tea, which was poured out by the hostess, who stood by the table, her guests around her.

One felt at home. One exchanged ideas with no apparent reticences on all possible subjects. "Courtesy" did not prevent, at times, Rabelaisian or naughty stories. It was a gathering open to ideas, discoursing at length on the topics of the day, the talent of those who were absent, and praising the talent of those present.

Arnold was in his element in that crowd. He loved to mix with them. The house was fascinating. Arnold, who hated long evenings, went there often and came home late at night.

"You can't, somehow, get away from them," he would say. "They don't know when to go to bed . . . any more than they know when to get up. Some of those talented men round there will ruin themselves if they are not careful."

I thought, "What about you, my boy?"

I candidly confess that I was rather jealous of that fascinating woman, who was not beautiful but who possessed great charm. Her gestures, her way of listening to you, the monotony of her caressing voice expressed mystery. She was

73

Slav and had the charm of her race. She was
fond of music. She was cultured, crafty and
clever in many ways. She was a woman (though
married) that married women, not knowing her
well, feared. For a woman generally fears her
intellectual superior. Arnold little suspected I
feared her influence on him. He came to know
of it.

After his success in America he was able to
realize the dream of his life, to be the owner of
a yacht. He acquired the "Velsa."

We still had, at the time, our house in Fontainebleau. These friends had a country house
two miles off, where they spent a few months in
the summer. I remember both of us sitting on
the sofa of our drawing-room one fine day in
early summer. Arnold was talking about his
recent acquisition the yacht "Velsa," bought
at Richmond a fortnight before—a nice, roomy
boat. He had talked about her to Monsieur
and Madame X. who had been most impressed.
My back turned, they had pulled strings to their
own advantage.

Arnold seated near me on the sofa, said,
looking at the lovely sky framed by the French
window which opened into the garden, "I
have asked Monsieur and Madame X. to sail
with me as you are not a good sailor."

"What!" I exclaimed.

74

Arnold said, "They have accepted."

"Have they indeed! Whether I am sick while at sea or not, I am going too!"

I expect the tone of my voice, the expression on my face expressed the feelings which were raging in me, for Arnold, very gently, short of breath, his eyes glittering, surprised and happy, said, "You don't mean it?"

"Yes, I do."

"Silly girl, I did not suspect you would feel it like that. . . . All right, my child, they shall not come."

What an unexpected tenderness!

They did not come.

I never knew if my dear husband had actually asked them to join him before he referred to it, but I know I did value the extent of his love for me.

He added, "You need not fear any woman."

What a comfort and what confidence in myself I had the right to have after such a delightful scene!

VI

CERTAIN of his love for me I was. It did not
prevent me from being very sensitive when he
was abrupt and cutting. I did not realize to the
full, at the time, that one of the two of us had
to adapt themselves to the other's ways and
leadership. It is impossible to give and take in
the same balance, as I thought it possible then.
Under the circumstances it was my place to give
up in trifles as well as in big things.

It was not the fact of having to do what
Arnold wished that made me rebel or hesitate,
it was the dictatorial way he expressed himself.
The tone of his voice was too dogmatic, too
imperative, to be interpreted in the right way
by me, a member of the Latin race. I had not
foreseen that a husband who loved you could
be sharp with you. It was very stupid of me.
. . . I could not help feeling hurt while
adaptation took place. I expected too much.
Time alone can heal the wound made by the
lack of perfection in human nature. Arnold's
kindness of heart, his zest for life, was the balm
which soothed hurts.

After we had been married a few years
Arnold wanted to organize our life on a new

plan. Before we gave up our small house in Fontainebleau, he said, "I want you to decide. It is either a big flat in Paris or a house in the country in England."

I was aghast. I having to choose! It made me responsible for the consequences . . . the effect his new surroundings would have on his work.

Seeing that he meant it, I asked for two days to make up my mind. As a matter of fact, in my subconscious mind, while talking, I thought of the danger Paris would be to him who needed peace for writing. I reflected that Monsieur and Madame X. and Paris would ruin his health and his talent. My impulse was to answer, "A flat in Paris, of course!" but my reason was prompting, "Give yourself time to make up your mind."

After two days I said to Arnold, "I would rather have a house in England."

"All right. We shall settle, as I said, in the country, and be there for many years to come."

I did not mind. I wanted to help the artist in him, to see his name in the public eye. I wanted him to realize his dreams to the full, and to maintain the place he had acquired for himself in English literature. I did not want any woman, any man, to ruin his talent by leading him astray and taking him away from me. England was the place for him. Having written

The Old Wives' Tale, Clayhanger and *Buried Alive*,
and having produced the plays *Cupid and Commonsense*, *The Honeymoon*, and above all the remarkable play *Milestones* (in collaboration with
Edward Knoblock), which had brought him
high prestige, to my mind his duty was to do
even better.

The play, *Milestones*, brings back to my
memory one of the happiest periods of our
married life. It was written in the summer of
1911 in Fontainebleau. The small garden in
front of the house had patches of brilliant colour,
geraniums, carnations, hyacinths, amongst
many other kinds of flowers—all responsible for
the brilliant rainbow of colour round the house.
Trees were giving shade to the house and to the
garden. At the back was a kitchen garden
shaded by fruit trees. A kiosk, Chinese in shape,
faced the French window of the drawing-room
and was not far from the kitchen. I have already
referred to it. We seemed to live in it. It was the
place where we had our meals, where tea was
served.

It was in that kiosk that Edward Knoblock
and Arnold Bennett used occasionally to have
tea together. Edward Knoblock came to the
Villa des Néfliers every afternoon. He did so
for many weeks running. Arnold showed him
the work he had done in the morning on the

play. Both worked regularly, conscientiously, efficiently and enthusiastically on the play, whose subject fascinated them both. It was beautiful to see these two men getting on splendidly. Keen and yet calm. One of them with perfect experience of the technique of the stage. The other, Arnold, happy to work with such a technician in an art he wanted to master completely.

The collaboration was in every way a huge success. It gave my husband immense pleasure to write that play. Every morning, every evening, he was exuberant about the scenes he had to write or had already written. He believed in the play and in the man who was collaborating with him. Everything went smoothly round us.

No title was found for the play before it was finished, nor was it found for a few days afterwards. It spoilt Arnold's pleasure in the work he had done. Many titles were suggested. I was asked to suggest one. I could but find the most banal titles. Arnold shrugged his shoulders or waved his beautiful hand in despair and repeated, "It is almost a cliché."

The afternoon the title was found we had ordered a carriage to visit the forest of Fontainebleau with friends. It was a hot afternoon. Coming back home Arnold suddenly exclaimed, "I have got it!"

"Got what?" asked one of our visitors.

I knew what he meant. I asked, anxious to know, "What title, then?"

"Yes, I have got it . . . it is a splendid one. It will do. I wonder why I did not think of it before. *Milestones*, that is to be the title."

He explained that he had been struck by the colour of the last milestone on the main road. This fact had inspired him. *Milestones* was adopted unanimously. It created curiosity.

The first night of the play was a triumph. Edward Knoblock and his sister witnessed it at the Royalty Theatre, March 6th, 1912. Arnold, extremely nervous, did not wish to be present. A wire sent to Fontainebleau, signed "Edward," intimated to us that its reception had surpassed expectations.

"I am relieved," said Arnold, "for one never knows with plays."

Arnold had at that period written over two dozen plays—most refused by different managers. But he had, in 1908, the joy of having his play, *Cupid and Commonsense* (adapted by himself from his novel, *Anna of the Five Towns*), produced by The Stage Society. He wrote that play on the absolute condition that it should be produced, so disgusted was he to have written over two dozen unproduced plays. But an admirer of his, Mr. Lee Mathews, a member of The Stage

Society, insisted that Arnold should try again.
He had great difficulty before he actually per-
suaded Arnold to follow his advice. He promised
Arnold the play would be produced for certain.
It was the beginning of Arnold's success in
drama.

After *Cupid and Commonsense* he wrote *The
Honeymoon*, then he wrote *What the Public Wants*
(1909)—both produced with success. That is to
say, he had had three first nights before *Milestones* was produced. These first nights were not
to see Arnold in the theatre. . . . No, he could
not stand the strain of it. He declared he "did
not mind a scrap" if the play were a success or
not; yet he was so nervous that he could not
face the strain such an experience would impose
upon him. He deliberately chose not to be
present. In the box reserved for the author
there was only me, his wife, to be seen, with
some of Arnold's relatives and friends. Arnold
on those nights had dinner with me, saw me
leave the house dressed for the occasion, smiling
and happy—yet, like him, very nervous—and
would then join an old friend of his, a journalist,
John Atkins, and spend the evening with him.
They begged me to meet them directly the
show was over at *Le Café de Paris*, where they
both waited, patiently or impatiently, to see me
enter the place.

"Here she is," Arnold would say, getting up to welcome me. "Well, then?"

John would listen to my enchantment, my enthusiasm, making out what he could, while Arnold, after I had finished my report of the evening, would say, "I knew it all from the expression on your face when you entered the café!"

They bade me drink and eat whatever I wished to order. I intentionally kept describing the enthusiasm, the fits of laughter and emotion. Having read the play and been to many of the rehearsals I knew it almost by heart.

These first nights moved me to the extent of being cold with fear of failure and hot with the realization of success.

VII

The money Arnold made out of the plays was, at my suggestion, used to repair the house, "Comarques," to furnish it and ultimately to buy it, after we had lived in it for a year.

It was a very old house. A house which appealed to Arnold chiefly because of the address.

"Think of it," he kept saying. " 'Comarques, Thorpe-le-Soken, Essex.' What an address! Do you like the house, Marguerite?"

"Yes, I do. . . . I feel at home here and you love it?"

"I do," said Arnold. "But a lot of money has to be spent to have it fixed, my dear."

I knew that Arnold meant to have central heating, running water, bathrooms, electric light, etc. Since his journey to America he craved more than ever to have perfect comfort, lavishness in clean linen, etc. Had he taken any other house he would have spent a lot of money on it just the same. So we decided to have the repairs done.

It was Edwin Rickards, the architect, Arnold's intimate friend, who did the work. It was done promptly, perfectly.

We had left France for good, but we had fixed ourselves in a healthy resort, in a lovely house with lovely grounds.

We possessed a car and the yacht "Velsa."

Arnold loved the place. It did him good. And I soon recovered from the trouble with my nerves which was affecting my heart in an alarming manner . . . faintness. I owe much to the climate of Essex; and to my husband, the memory of a home, which I adored for over seven years. A home which I thought he would never get rid of. But Arnold was Arnold. He did not crave for tranquillity, a fixed home. Having secured one he could not keep it for long. His constitution prevented him from being conservative. I was the constant, the conservative one of the two. "Comarques" meant everything to me. When it was decided to sell it, it broke my heart. It was one of the biggest tragedies of my life. I had dreamt that "Comarques" would be, like Shakespeare's home, a *lieu de pèlerinage*, when we should have both departed. The fact remains we left it for years.

After my husband's death I wished to have a tablet to his memory in Thorpe Church. It could not be done. Therefore I asked Lord and Lady Fairfax for their permission to place one on that house.

I am grateful to them, and to Canon Tollington, for their sympathy and understanding of my desire, and their help in obtaining my object.

VIII

"Comarques"! Seven years of our life were spent there. Seven years, during which the house was made use of, to our joy and the joy of many. Up-to-date arrangements made of this very old house a delicious, luxurious house. Well organized, well run, with a true feeling of hospitality, created by Arnold (and by me, his wife, if I may say so), our visitors felt at home directly they entered the door. French furniture, English freedom vied with each other in our Georgian house, supposed to have been built, at the time of the Revocation of the *Édit de Nantes*, by a French family called Comarques.

It was the very house for a couple who were of different nationality—one of them entirely British; born in the Midlands, in an industrial district; descended from potters, miners and tradespeople. The other one born in a small town of the old province *le Quercy*, in the south of France; descended from landowners and tradespeople. One brought up and trained in his family. The other spending her youth in school, trained by strangers. Both of them trained by the best master, Life. Both of them partly self-made . . . highly strung . . . re-

ligiously brought up, conscientiously trust-
worthy, disliking liars, suspicious of over-polite
people, out to help, out to give pleasure, ready
to respond to kindness, valuing kindness, valuing people and material things. In two words,
loving life. Fighters and workers, each in his
own sphere.

I did not realize my own character at the
time I married Arnold Bennett, nor did I for
a few years afterwards; but Arnold, himself,
made me know myself.

"You are too retiring, too modest, too much
of an idealist. The day you come to know yourself you will be a great woman. Whatever hap-
pens to you, you will always be dignified. No
fear that you will ruin yourself . . . no fear
that people will lose money through you.
Not only are you anxious to pay your bills
but you will worry if bills are not sent to
you. You are a funny woman, you know,
Marguerite!"

"Darling, I am out for security."

"Yes, I know. As for me I like risk . . . life
with no risks would not be life at all. Risks,
debts are stimulating to me."

"Yes, yes, because you believe you will
always make money."

"Why shouldn't I?"

"Because no one can be certain that they

will not be handicapped through illness or in other ways."

"You are a pessimist!"

"No, no, my boy, I am wise!"

"So am I."

"Of course you are."

"Don't worry, my child, rely on me," was Arnold's conclusive saying.

I did rely on him. He saw to the money-making. He knew much better than I how to make good. My part was to go on helping him by being what I was, a helpful companion, a good hostess to our guests.

"Comarques"! How Arnold enjoyed the house, the garden, his study, his bedroom! How happy he was to walk round the grounds so as to learn what the head gardener had to tell him, to convince him that, with little expense, he could continually improve our beautiful garden! How proud he was to walk on his own lawn, which was like a carpet bought by the yard and sewn together for him to walk on! How happy I was when by a mere chance I caught him strolling into the garden just for the pleasure of strolling!

I would say, "Are not the flowers beautiful?"

"Very . . . what are they?"

I would say in the kitchen garden, "Arnold, look! the carrots will soon be ready for the table."

Arnold Bennett chatting in the garden of the
California Hotel, Cannes, in 1911, to
Marguerite Mayol, Author of "Twin Beds."

Arnold would say, "You mean the green leaves are carrots?"

He could not tell what carrot, turnip or radish leaves were like. He was not interested in botany, agriculture, in animals or in flowers. He came from an industrial district.

It was in my blood to be enthusiastic about anything coming out of the soil and about any animals. Acute pleasure was rooted in me at the sight of the fields, the trees, the sky. I was an enthusiast and a dreamer. I was the owner of an infinitesimal particle of the earth, yet it made no impression on me walking on my very own estate, so much in love was I with the very earth I was walking on.

Alas! my fundamental joy was spoilt by the fact that the head gardener made us feel the garden belonged to him first. It was to me unbelievable that a man paid for his work could prevent me from picking my own flowers, from picking fruit, green peas or whatever I wished to pick. By his attitude he spoilt the joy I derived from the garden. Happily he could not deprive me of the joy that the house gave me. Arnold found no fault with the gardener, in common with many owners of gardens requiring head gardeners. However, he ended by finding out, after many years, that he had trusted the man too blindly. I must say, till his

discharge, he kept the place in beautiful order
and was very industrious. He knew that his
master could not tell the name of a plant and
he took advantage of his ignorance.

There is an anecdote which I cannot help
telling. An oldish lady, a friend of ours, born
in South Africa, was staying at "Comarques"
with us, while her husband was in South Africa
on examination work. She knew how fond of
the garden I was. We had both noticed fig trees
grew very well in that part of the East Coast;
as did the peach, apricot and nectarine trees
which I had had planted against the brick wall
of the kitchen garden, and which were covered
that year with fruit.

I remarked to her, "I would like a fig tree in
this place."

She said, "I would ask the gardener if I
were you."

"Yes, but it is like this . . . he will not do
it if Arnold does not tell him as well!"

"All right, ask Arnold to tell him."

"Somehow I don't think I like bothering
him with the garden and the fig tree just yet.
He is finishing a book. Besides, there is no
hurry."

"All right," she said. "I will tell Arnold for
you."

She was a sort of elderly sister to my husband,

and I thought, being English, she knew what she was doing.

Arnold joined us at tea in the garden. Mrs. Sharpe, that was her name, said, "Arnold, Marguerite would like a fig tree in the kitchen garden."

"All right," said Arnold, "she shall have one."

He asked the parlourmaid to call the head gardener.

"Yes, sir," said the man when in front of us.

"Tom, I would like you to plant a fig tree in the garden."

"Yes, sir. They do grow in this part very well, sir. I will ask for seeds and grow one."

"For seeds!" exclaimed Mrs. Sharpe. "But, Arnold, it will take years before it becomes a small tree, and we may be dead before it bears fruit! It is not a question of seeds. Buy a three-year-old tree, as you have done for the other fruit trees you have added to the garden."

"What do you think of it, Tom?"

"Well, sir, to grow a fig tree from seeds would be cheaper."

"You may order a fig tree," said Arnold, dismissing the man.

The gardener disappeared. Were men's ears the same shape as horses', and with the same mobility, the gardener's ears would have shown anger. His back certainly did.

When he was out of sight Mrs. Sharpe said, "That man is the limit. I would not have believed it possible. He took you for a fool. Arnold, I thought I heard you say that he is intelligent!"

Mrs. Sharpe had to pay for her courage.

A few days later she and I were in the kitchen garden. We were picking green peas and eating them on the spot. We had picked a few and eaten them when the gardener saw us from the green-house or from some other part where we could not see him. The next day he said to his master that we had been eating green peas that he had sown for seeds.

We caught it from Arnold, but Mrs. Sharpe said, "The man is mad. There are rows and rows of peas. What does it mean?"

The fact was the gardener disliked me.

Not being a horse, Arnold's ears did not move, but he was speechless and made no remark. When the season came for it the fig tree was planted.

IX

THERE was a pond by the lawn in front of the
house. It was very tempting to have ducks
floating on it. I could not resist the temptation,
so we bought a few. There was plenty of food
for rabbits. I could not resist having a few. As
for cats, they mysteriously appeared on the
scene. Naturally I had a dog to talk to; a pet
dog, a Pekinese, that I had bought from Mrs.
E. V. Lucas, who bred them at that time near
Brighton. I called him Raton. Then we had a
fox-terrier called John.

I loved my ducks, my rabbits, my cats and
my dogs. They knew me. I could do what I
liked with them. The ducks would come on to
my knee to be fed . . . they were beautiful.
Some were white. Others had lovely colours as
though painted with a brush. These ducks, as
soon as the sun brought the daylight again,
would make as much noise as a motor-horn in
a town. Their hideous noise did not add to their
charm for me, but they reminded me every
morning of the blessing which was our lot . . .
the beautiful spot where we lived. But, either
in his bedroom or at his desk in the early morning, Arnold would be cursing the ducks for

annoying him with their exasperating "honk, honk." He at first referred to them gently . . . not showing me that they angered him. I loved my ducks so much that the thought of losing them did not cross my mind.

I had noticed that some among them did not make so much noise as others did. I asked an old man working under the head gardener how it was.

He said, "The ones making so much noise are the females. You can scarcely hear the males!"

This revelation inspired me with the right solution of the problem, so as to abolish the source of Arnold's morning disturbance and to enable me to keep ducks for my pleasure and as a decoration for the pond.

"We shall have only drakes," I thought.

I hunted the country round in my car, driving myself, in order to buy drakes only.

"Are you sure they are males?"—when they were shown to me.

"Yes, mam."

"Very well, make sure you only bring me drakes, and please bring them to me when a little older to 'Comarques,' Thorpe."

"Yes, mam."

I was never asked why I wanted male birds only . . . but I knew that I interested them with my drakes and my French accent!

Having secured enough males to charm our eyes and spare our ears, I felt happier, for Arnold would be pleased; to disturb him in the early morning he would have only the singing of the birds and the cockerel's hymn to the sun. I wanted to give Arnold a surprise.

It was he who gave me a surprise two days later, on market day.

At breakfast he said to me, "I have given orders that the ducks are to be taken to the market to-day and sold."

It gave me a shock.

"Please don't have all of them sold."

"Yes, they must go . . . as a matter of fact, they are not on the pond any longer."

I told him about drakes being almost mute.

"Very well," he said, "have males if you like, but if they happen to be females they will have to go."

Males, only males, were seen for years on our pond.

A couple of swans were added to them. The first pair was offered to us by a theatre manager wanting to please Arnold. They flew away. A second couple was offered to me by an officer staying with us during the war. That second couple of swans had a tragic end.

X

HARDLY had we settled at "Comarques" before we began having visitors at the week-ends. The first friend to come was Rickards, the architect. Arnold as a bachelor had lived with him at one time. He was a most engaging and interesting guest. Arnold refused to ask anybody else for the first week-end he was with us. I was asked to criticize the work he had done in the house. He had helped us choose the wallpaper and some of the furniture. He, who was a bachelor living in two rooms in London, was for the first time in his life asked to stay in a private house of the style of "Comarques." He, having been Arnold's intimate friend for years, took it as a matter of course that our country home would be, to a certain extent, his. He was eager to come often. He did so.

It was a big order to criticize what Arnold's beloved and clever friend had achieved. I only wanted to criticize the amount of money he had made us spend on the house—this, because it came to one-third more than Rickards had said. Arnold begged me not to refer to the expense. I did not, but I pointed out to Rickards that, though everything else he had done in the house was, to my mind, perfect, he had forgotten to make use of the space which was under the roof of our house.

I said, "It puzzles me, Rickards, why you did not trouble about the second storey?"

"Dear me, what else do you want? There is in that attic a bathroom, two servants' rooms and a spare room. You don't need anything else. Have you not got enough rooms?"

"No," I said. "Arnold needs two for his own use: his bedroom and his study, close by; and I also need two rooms for my own use: my bedroom, beside Arnold's, and another room as a boudoir. You have turned one of the bedrooms into a bathroom, another into a study for Arnold's secretary . . . don't you see there are only two spare rooms left in the house?"

"That is true," said Arnold.

"It can't be helped," Rickards said. "Besides, it would have cost a lot more to turn the attic into passages and bedrooms."

Arnold would have let the matter drop. He did not want more spare rooms, I knew. I begged him to let me see what a local architect would charge to carry out my idea about turning the attic into another floor.

"Would you mind?" Arnold asked Rickards.

"Why should I? Marguerite has a good idea. Local people should be able to do it cheaply."

It was done and Rickards approved of it and said the charge made was very small.

So it was that we had four spare rooms instead of two. The best one was on the first floor, above the kitchen. It was supposed to be haunted . . . but I did not know that at first. It was the room many of my friends in turn occupied.

We began having a succession of visitors; all Arnold's friends or disciples. Mr. James Pinker, his literary agent; Mr. George Doran, his American publisher; Frank Swinnerton, his disciple; Hugh Walpole, another young admirer and disciple. Mrs. Belloc Lowndes came. Mr. E. V. Lucas came.

I have always suspected that he saw the ghost in the double spare room he occupied, for, the morning after his arrival, he found an excuse to shorten his visit, which was to last three days. Did he see Comarques' ghost? I never did, and I slept one night in that room before any visitor ever had! I slept in every spare room before any of our friends did, for I wanted to see for myself if there was anything lacking for their comfort.

After E. V. Lucas shortened his visit, I told every friend occupying this room, "If you hear strange noises during the night you will know it is due to the pipes in the kitchen and possibly to cats and rats strolling on the roof above your head."

I had explained the strange noise I had heard when half asleep in that way to myself. I am not one to believe absolutely in ghosts, though I saw one once while in my twenties. An extraordinary figure of a man, coming through the wall in a phosphorescent cloud. I was just awakening and certainly not dreaming. The vision appeared two mornings running. I saw nothing of that sort at "Comarques," nor ever since.

Arnold did not believe in ghosts, though he wrote a book called *The Ghost*.

I think I make no mistake in saying that E. V. Lucas does—or did at that time—believe in ghosts. He was a strange visitor. Very silent . . . dreamy . . . looking absently at Arnold and at me. Perhaps he did not feel at home with me, or perhaps he was composing a poem while sitting at our table—a poem which I have never read, though I love poetry.

Arnold liked Lucas. He would say, "He is a funny chap . . . but he has a heart of gold. He is kind and sentimental without being sugary."

Like many of our visitors, he talked about books. It was at the time obscure to me, but never boring.

99

Arnold used to say, "We are talking shop, and Marguerite can't follow."

"I will one day," I used to remark.

Arnold would smile, as if questioning this.

I would afterwards occasionally say, when such a conversation had been going on for a long while, for I could not follow English spoken at that speed, "Here you are talking shop again!"

Arnold was amused, for he did not realize that I had grasped the full meaning of the expression.

Arnold hardly ever explained anything to me. I had to find out English customs (which on the whole are topsy-turvy to those of France) for myself. I had to manage as well as I could and do everything on my own initiative. I made endless *faux pas*. No end of complications and misunderstandings arose from my ignorance of the language and mentality of a race which was unknown to me. It follows that I must have been most amusing or irritating to others at times. As for me, I was learning to stand on my own feet and to make the best of everything, and to try to please everybody. But my good intentions brought appalling consequences at times. However, they were not of a devastating character.

Arnold also lived in a world of his own, though

having, with me, an element of great interest in our friends. He was exacting in the house as in everything. He could be exasperatingly exacting, but he inspired method and efficiency by his good example.

I was never bored in our house. No visitors bored me; on the contrary, I enjoyed everything and everyone. I felt at home with all and behaved freely. I poured out on them an extraordinary language which they pretended to understand. I took it they knew what I meant, as I guessed from their answers and remarks. I am inclined to think that none of them were bored, for I was a sort of circus to them all.

It used to amuse Arnold greatly. He would say when we were in the privacy of our room, "You do say and do strange things . . . they do not mind, as you are French. It is all so funny!"

"Yes, *cheri*, you should correct me."

"No fear! Were I to start you would have to learn English all over again. I have not time."

No! ah no! he had not time. Regular creative work and other things occupied him; resting every day after lunch, going for walks, playing tennis, reading books, writing books and articles, his journal, writing letters, criticizing novels to help beginners or to please himself—

thousands of activities all done methodically, with enthusiasm and keenness.

No! he had not time for Marguerite, for his wife. He felt sorry for her, but it could not be helped. She knew he deplored it; but Arnold had resigned himself to the fact.

An artist always ends by putting his work first, his wife second. His creation is his beloved mistress—a tyrannical, irresistible mistress. Can anyone wonder that an artist's wife is, at times, jealous of her husband's work? I presume that wives of business men think their husband's work is a tyrant, too. It is said that work alone gives pure satisfaction, therefore why have we the illusion that love, kindness, devotion, or affection will give one complete satisfaction? Nothing does give complete satisfaction. One either possesses a contented mind or one does not.

Arnold trained himself to have a contented mind; to do good when the chance arose; to do what he wanted, because he had had that privilege almost all his life and was in a position to do so, because he knew what his wishes were. He was friendly with everybody and commanded respect. Servants were devoted to him and would do anything for him. His secretary, Miss Winifred Nerney, foresaw his needs, loved to work for him and enjoyed his charm and his

authority. She was treated by him with consideration and courtesy. She was always rewarded generously for her work, which she did
devotedly from 1913 until the day of his death,
27th March, 1931. She was the axis of his
"shop," almost of his life. He had no secret
from her, whom he treated as a human being
as well as a machine. She was the very secretary
for him. She had in him, to start with, not only
an employer, but one who knew the art of
being an efficient secretary as well.

Tidiness was one of his first principles.

One of his remarks was, "One can never be
too particular about one's own job."

He knew how to give orders because he knew
how the orders ought to be carried out. Having been an employee himself, he knew that
the most conscientious worker has lapses and
makes slips. He was indulgent, but the lapses
and slips were noticed by him. He would either
keep willingly silent about them or refer to
them. In either case his authority was felt, and
only a fool would imagine that he had not
noticed carelessness and neglect as clearly as
perfection in work. A scrutinizing eye he had.

Anyone entering many spheres of activity
requires the help of other people. It follows
that one has to shut one's eyes at times. Perfection does not exist.

XI

ARNOLD, wide-awake though he was, was pretty often deceived by people, and many took advantage of his kindness of heart—his impulsive moods making him promise help, money and protection.

He has helped many. He has for years and years given a big or a small pension to old people not related to him, as well as to members of his own family. At the time he was just beginning to make good he saved from humiliation, from prison, a man whose weakness, lack of decency, and crookedness had gradually ruined his business and his household. Yes, Arnold, having no savings, made himself responsible for a huge sum of money to save the man. He did not shrink from the risk he undertook. We had huge expenses at the time and also quite enough responsibility as it was. Having bound himself to do a thing he did it, never grumbling, never referring to it. But I think he imposed on those he was saving from humiliation and starvation that they must behave themselves in future.

I did admire his generosity. He had, however, the pettiness that most intellectual people of his type have. He was so amusingly mean in trifles. It was charming to see this childish sight in him. There is a Gascon saying which I have to translate in my mind from the patois into French, and from French into English: "Throwing away the flour and using the bran." It could be applied to my husband.

XII

To my way of thinking, and to my despair, we were throwing away flour and bran from the beginning of Arnold's success. We had the yacht "Velsa." He spared no money on her. We had a crew of three men. We started for Holland. We had a visitor on board, Rickards. We had everything just so. It was lovely and we did enjoy the freedom we had.

Arnold stood at the wheel for hours. He wrote his journal, which took the form of essays and was afterwards published under the title of *The Log of the "Velsa."* It is written in printed characters, with hardly any corrections, and it is beautifully bound in an antique binding of the eighteenth century. This piece of art protects the wonderful handwriting of a great writer who had the gift to put down what he saw and felt in a most illuminating way with the patience of a monk.

The Log of the "Velsa," as a book, was illustrated by Edwin Rickards, who was an artist and whose work was greatly admired by Arnold Bennett.

Both of them competed in drawing and water colour at the time we were visiting Dutch towns and little villages.

When Arnold was writing or resting in the afternoon he would say, "You two go on shore and please yourselves. There is a lot to be seen."

He knew that I, like his friend Rickards (with whom I got on very well), loved exploring villages to discover the market-place and the church; to go into the shops; to observe the streets and the inhabitants. Rickards discoursed to me at great length on the different styles of architecture. He loved to point out Dutch girls, to compare them with English, French and Italian girls he had met and known. He was amused by my keenness on any subject, at my wonderful patience to listen to his exhaustive conversation about people I did not know. He made up for Arnold, who spoke but little. Arnold was the best listener of the three of us, as most silent people are. I was not such a good listener as he. My mind would wander about, especially when getting tired of listening to a language which hid at the time so much of its subtle and profound meaning for me.

It was said about Rickards by some of his friends and acquaintances, "He is a bore. So thoroughly engrossed in himself."

Arnold would say, "He is the most interesting man I know. I never find him a bore."

Rickards was not a bore to me. I owe him

many delightful hours. He was nice to Arnold and me. His affection for Arnold gave him the right to tell Arnold what he thought of him, with his extreme fussiness about small things and particularly about punctuality for meals.

"Are you aware you are spoiling pleasure?"

Arnold would say, "Never mind. Go ashore with Marguerite and be sure to be back at twelve; not a minute later!"

I was charmed to hear them.

While Rickards would say, "Marguerite, you should cure Arnold of his tyrannical ways."

I retorted, "You lived with him for years before I ever met him. Why did you not cure him of it yourself?"

"It is not the same," said Rickards. "Women accomplish miracles."

I did not accomplish that miracle anyway— and I am not sure that I wanted to cure him of his mania for exactitude. It was a good habit which I valued.

XIII

The "Velsa" was again to be our floating home in the spring of 1914. She was sent through the French canals to Marseilles. From there Arnold started on her alone, along the coast of the French Riviera and the Italian coast to Rome.

We had planned to do the journey back from Rome to Calais in our car, so as to gain time. We also had had the car sent to Paris. From Paris our English chauffeur drove us to Marseilles. There I was left alone with him, as he could not speak either French or Italian. Arnold and I were to meet every evening at a fixed port. The first one to arrive was to wait for the other.

This enchanting racing lasted up to Piombino. The car arrived twenty-eight hours before the yacht. I was not without anxiety about it. I found rooms in the only possible hotel in the place . . . a room for the chauffeur and a room for myself.

There was a circus at night in the public square. I said to the chauffeur, "I would like you to walk to the circus with me and come back to meet me."

"Yes, madam."

"Would you like to see the show?"

"Yes, madam."

"All right. I will get a ticket for you as well."

I saw that the man was pleased.

He respectfully sat a few seats away from me, but we walked to the circus together and left it together.

When I told Arnold he said, "People must be intrigued with that chauffeur of yours!"

Then we made for Naples. Again we arrived three hours before the "Velsa." I asked my chauffeur to take me to the port and to go back to the hotel where I had just booked a room for him and a place for the car in the garage.

"Yes, madam."

The chauffeur looked at me as though asking, "What are you going to do with yourself meanwhile?"

I had thought it a fine idea to hire a dinghy to go out to meet the "Velsa" and my husband. But it was not a fine idea at all. Hardly had I left the shore with the three men who manned the small boat when the harbour master, who spoke English, told the chauffeur, "Your mistress should not have gone with those men. They are suspicious characters. Foreigners have been missed and never seen again. One has to be careful."

The chauffeur told my husband this. Afterwards he was told the same thing by the harbour master. Arnold said to me, "You have no sense of danger. One of these days you will be assassinated. . . . You should not do things like that."

He was decidedly angry with me. I did not tell him that I had had reason to fear assassination by these men, and that my salvation was due to my presence of mind and the arrival of the "Velsa" at the psychological moment.

We wanted to visit the two famous islands, Elba (where Napoleon was exiled for a time) and Corsica (the island of his birth). It was not for these reasons we wished to visit these two places. It was just to see what they were like. We arrived at Elba after a good crossing. We landed under a beautiful sun. I had the definite impression of landing on another planet.

Close to the harbour, which is small, there was a restaurant. Very gay, clean and made gayer by bottles of wine (shaped like round decanters, with round bodies and very long necks) which were frilled with coloured paper of various tints. They made a most strikingly decorative effect. There were many plans to welcome visitors and to invite them to enter the restaurant and have a good meal. We had our cook . . . restaurants did not see our money (except at Rome).

Being on shore, and having time before our meal, Arnold suggested a walk. I was all for it. We had to take the only road which led to the house Napoleon had lived in, some distance off. I noticed the absence of traffic. There came along a cart with a labourer and his family. They saluted us. Arnold made remarks about them; none about the island. He looked absorbed.

I said, "It will be interesting to visit Napoleon's house."

"I am not going anyway," he said. "We did not come to this island to visit any house. We came for the night, with the idea of starting to-morrow morning for Corsica, wind permitting."

"But surely we have time to do that much?"

"Visit the house if you like. As for me I have no wish to go."

Saying so, he turned back and I alone visited the historical place. My pleasure and interest were somewhat spoiled, my mind dwelling on Arnold's strange absence of interest in the enchanting Elba and the famous house of a famous man.

Next morning we made for Corsica, but the

wind did not permit us to get there. We had
to put back to Elba. Next day the same thing
happened. Arnold gave up the idea of going
to Corsica. We had lost two days, and I
suffered endless horrors from the agonies of
seasickness.

We had a most interesting and enjoyable trip.
I have a very vivid picture of it all.

One day the yacht entered the Tiber and
travelled up to Rome with the help of her
paraffin engine. We anchored there. It created
a great sensation. Perhaps a Dutch yacht had
not been seen on the Tiber for years.

It was at Rome that we dismissed the car and
gave the chauffeur a few days' holiday. He did
not know what to do with himself. That young
Englishman took no interest in ruins or
museums, not even in cafés. He felt lost and as
if all Italy were inhabited by criminals, thieves
and contaminated people. He felt safer with
the crew of the "Velsa." The day we left Rome
for Paris he looked younger than ever, cleaner
than ever and neater than any chauffeur in
Rome.

Arnold, also, was pleased to leave the place.
His interest in it was exhausted. He could take
things in very quickly. He was very observant.
He had a good memory and he had the gift of
spotting at once what many would never see.

His intelligence was exceptional. His active
brain could not rest. He was not curious about
details, yet he vividly described what he had
seen and felt.

XIV

On our return to Paris I had to see a doctor. He called in a specialist. Both tried to convince me to go at once to the specialist's nursing home to be operated upon. I refused, for the good reason that I could not let my husband go back to our English home, which would be disorganized after our long absence. "He is to start a new book. When he is in the swim of it and the house is running smoothly, and if I am not better, after carefully following your advice, I will come back. I promise."

The doctor answered, "Patients say things like that but they forget."

I repeated, "If I am not better in a month's time, I shall let you know and go to your nursing home."

The doctors saw I had made up my mind to follow my husband.

As a matter of fact I preceded him to "Comarques" by two days. He found the house organized and flowers everywhere. On his writing-table, in a small red vase, he found a few chosen flowers. He was pleased but not surprised, for from the very beginning of our married life I was in the habit of putting a few

flowers on the right side of his writing-desk. I
felt they would inspire him, help him, comfort
him.

If I saw little of him these flowers saw much.
Moveless, beautiful and perfumed, they were
the incarnation of the femininity which my
husband feared in me, because of its possible
devastating consequences. He did not realize
that with my well-balanced mind I would see
to that. I had to "see to that." I was the dyke
restraining the overflowing of his passion . . .
the tender nurse, inspiring respect, bringing
peace to the exhausted man who was working
too hard and who occasionally had break-
downs. Did I not bless God that I, out of all
women alive, was given the mission of looking
after and nursing that great man? For England's
sake I wanted him to be even greater. For the
love of him, for the glory of England and for the
prestige of Frenchwomen, I was ready to endure
whatever I should have to endure, from the
sick, nervy, fidgety, darling patient of mine.

Standing at the foot of his bed one day, I
said to him, "Darling, it is a blessing God sent
me to you!"

"Don't play me the trick of ever dying," he
answered.

XV

I DID not get better and arrangements were
made for me to return to France to be operated
on. Arnold took me to Thorpe-le-Soken station
—and I arrived in Paris, alone, late in the
evening. The nursing home was situated near
Paris, at Neuilly. I took a taxi and arrived there
about midnight.

The nurse, realizing who I was, asked,
"Where is your husband?"

"In England. I came over alone."

"Fancy you coming here alone! Where is
your maid?"

"I am alone," I repeated.

She could not get over the fact that a patient,
having to undergo an operation in two days'
time, had travelled alone from England to
Neuilly-sur-Seine.

It created a stir in this fashionable nursing
home. I became a sort of saint, married
to a cruel rich man. This legend I could not
destroy. How was it possible to make people
understand Arnold's attitude? He who hated
illness, nursing homes, anything which would
diminish his enthusiasm for life. He knew I was
in good hands. He spared no money for my

comfort. He knew that a doctor, his friend, would look after me. He knew my sister visited me daily. She brought me flowers, fruit and the news of the day.

On the 14th July—the French national day —she said, "Let me wheel your bed near the window. Aeroplanes are to fly over us. You should see them fly! Have you not heard the rumour that we will soon be at war?"

"Don't you believe it," I exclaimed. "Arnold says it can't be so . . . that we shall never see war again!"

"Arnold is not always right," she retorted.

"He generally is," I replied—and she left me convinced, through my own conviction, that Arnold was right.

In his daily letters he had never referred to war with Germany, but I knew his views. "Religious wars no longer exist. It is the same with wars between nations," I had heard him say very often.

XVI

A few days after I arrived back at " Comarques," Arnold broke the news to me that he had arranged to go to Dieppe on his yacht and to cruise along the French coast, via Biarritz, with a friend.

The news surprised me in a way, yet I understood that he wanted a change. Yachting was the best relaxation for him. He had benefited to such an extent on the previous occasion that it would have been selfish of me to make any remark about him going away so soon after I had come back.

It was decided he would leave "Comarques" at the very end of July and sail to Dieppe. I anxiously awaited to hear of his safe arrival, for the sea was rough. A few days later I had a wire from him, "Just arrived Dieppe. War declared with Germany. Coming back. Arnold."

The contents of his wire did not surprise me. My anxiety was not diminished. My anguish was great. War! France and Germany at war and I a Frenchwoman . . . and Arnold, my well-informed English husband, started on his voyage in spite of the rumour of war. What

119

would come next? England joining France? Arnold said, "No, it will not come to that. What would be gained by such unnecessary sacrifice?"

The newspapers were not big enough to pour out on the public the different and lengthy views.

"We should not go to war," said a famous politician.

"We should. We cannot help it," wrote a journalist.

Arnold and his like were certain England would not be so foolish. But a few days after Germany had declared war on France, England, loyal, strong, determined, generous and foreseeing, joined in the conflict.

The East Coast saw many troops camping along the seashore. Regiments passed our village under the burning heat that summer. Inhabitants massed themselves along the way, throwing fruit to the boys who were sure to be thirsty. From "Comarques" we started with baskets full of apples. I had a French niece and two French nephews staying with us at the time. They hurried curiously to the village, eager to see the English soldiers—and to spoil them.

Meanwhile Arnold was having his afternoon daily rest.

When we got back for tea we told him about these exciting events. He made no remark. He did not approve of it. To him the time was too serious. He was reflecting what he could possibly do to prevent the war going on. There was nothing to stop it.

From London came an appeal to do our bit for the Belgium refugees massed in England. We could not take any in, but Arnold sent a fat cheque to one of the committees dealing with them. A committee was formed in Putney. One of its active members was Mrs. Herbert Sharpe, our friend. She induced Arnold to become the president of that branch. He was a most efficient president.

I, from "Comarques," sent whatever I could . . . clothes Arnold had discarded; dresses, coats I could do without; . . . shoes . . . underclothing . . . everything I could collect in the house. From the garden we sent, weekly, a large hamper of fruit and vegetables. Arnold gave the fund a weekly cheque of £50.

Our financial position was secure and remained so throughout the war, for my husband had signed a contract in America for his next three books. We were among the fortunate ones.

When the cold weather came the soldiers and their officers had to be billeted for the winter.

General Fitzgerald, head of the staff at Frinton-on-Sea, called on us with his aide-de-camp, Lieutenant Trotter. We gave them tea. Their visit was a short one.

Lieutenant Trotter informed us that a detachment of engineers had arrived at Thorpe in the morning, that the men were billeted in the village and that there was one young officer who was rich and used to comfort who had to be satisfied with a room in a stuffy small cottage. He added that he thought himself lucky not to be worse off.

I looked at Arnold as though to say, "Let us ask him to stay here with us . . . plenty of room."

Arnold understood, and I ventured to say, "He might like to stay with us better?"

"That would be a kind deed," said the general.

"Not at all."

"When do you think you could have him, Mr. Bennett?"

"Whenever he likes."

"May I tell him?" asked the aide-de-camp.

"Do," said Arnold.

"Please ask him to come at once," I added.

"He will be grateful, I know," remarked Lieutenant Trotter.

When our visitors had departed I said to

Arnold, "I am so happy, Arnold; you do not mind that officer coming?"

"Why should I mind? . . . besides, it will give you something to do!"

I was longing to help those doing their duty towards their country.

The young officer, Lieutenant Grant Michaelis (East Anglian Royal Engineers), son of Mr. and Mrs. Edward Michaelis, stayed with us eight months. We had the chance to meet his people who were Australian and were staying at the Ritz. Their son left us to be sent to the front with his men. He was the first one billeted with us sent to the front, and the first one killed out of those we knew. Both Arnold and I felt his death badly. He had been such a nice companion. Arnold could talk intelligently to him. He appreciated anything done for him. He enjoyed our home without ostentation, which provided him with all the comfort and luxury he was accustomed to.

His people have ever since been most grateful for what we did for their dear boy during the war. Arnold's kindness made a great impression on them. They have remained my friends all these long years and I am extremely fond of them. They did not forget in their letters of sympathy to me on the sad death of my husband to point out his extreme kindness to the boy, any more than they have forgotten the beautiful letter he wrote to them when we heard the tragic news.

When that young officer left us for the front, I had said to Arnold, "Too nice, too intelligent to die! He should be spared."

Arnold's answer was, "You should add, too conscientious."

The boy had volunteered.

Before this young officer had left us we had other officers of the Royal Horse Artillery billeted with us. Their horses were in the stables. The men's horses in barns by the stables. One of their officers induced Arnold to ride one of their horses. Arnold had not ridden for thirteen years. The temptation was too great. It was arranged he should ride with a few of them to Frinton-on-sea, six miles off.

"You will feel sore for days afterwards," I told him.

"Nothing of the kind . . . a hot bath on my return will prevent it."

I was alarmed. I thought, "Stiff as my husband looks, being out of practice and nearly fifty years of age, he will not be able to keep his balance any longer."

I did not succeed in making him give up such a foolish enterprise. I said to one of the officers with whom I was friendly, "Please look after Arnold . . . I am afraid of an accident."

He was amused; I could see as much in his blue eyes, cold like steel. "Don't worry, Mrs. Bennett, I will look after him all right."

Somehow I did not think he would. I made up my mind to take my car out and to follow them to Frinton.

The horses went first and I followed driving the car. The officers were highly interested. Some of them would look back occasionally to see if I was still following their detachment. Arnold, stiff and straight, never turned his head. He did not realize I was following him with the car for him to use . . . as if it were an ambulance.

He led the march from the very start. When entering Frinton-on-sea in front of these smart, slim, well-turned-out officers, he looked like a proud general, dressed in civilian clothes. It was funny to see him. People recognized him and saluted him, but he did not acknowledge their salutes. He led his men to the sandy beach and I in my car could no longer follow him. He did not dismount and he returned to "Comarques" at the head of the cavalcade.

Back at home, Arnold asked, "Why did you follow me with the car? I knew nothing would happen. It was rather ridiculous, you know."

"I don't care. You are safe."

Arnold was proud to have done it. He said, getting into his hot bath, "They will not catch me again . . . besides, I have to go to London to-morrow."

He complained the next morning of lumbago, but set off in spite of it. Next day I had a letter, "I shall not be able to return home for a few days, my lumbago is worse," etc. . . .

He would not admit his lumbago was due to his having ridden after the years and years he had dropped it. Our guests sympathized with him about his lumbago and laughed up their sleeves.

"Mr. Bennett, when are you going to ride again?" asked my favourite officer, jokingly, a short time afterwards.

"Never," said Arnold. "I have not time."

"Of course not, sir."

Neither of them was deceived about the other.

XVII

Arnold did not volunteer. His age, his highly strung constitution were sufficient reasons to prevent him doing so. He was amongst those who were more useful out of the army than in it. His pen was his gun. His genius for organization found more scope on war committees than it would have in the trenches. No! Arnold was, above all, an intellectual. He would have been no good as a soldier. The only game he played was tennis. He was, in 1914, forty-eight years of age. He did not go to the front as a soldier (not even when conscription was established), but he was sent there as a journalist.

In 1915 he went to the trenches. He was nearly killed.

General Joffre and some of his staff received this *reporteur anglais*, Arnold Bennett, with the reverence due to an Englishman whose pen was expected to give heart to so many.

Arnold came back from the front with many photos taken of the battlefields. He also brought for me bits of a stained-glass window from Reims Cathedral. Treasures that I fully valued and that I still possess.

His visit to the front told on Arnold. His

nerves went all wrong. When back at "Comarques" he stayed in bed for days and days.
He had bad headaches. He attended to his
letters but wrote nothing for the time being.
The reality of war had affected him. He avoided
the subject. The officers billeted with us were
anxious to hear a full report of his impressions,
but he refused to talk about it. He said, "Read
my articles . . . you will know!"

His kindness, his generosity to all increased.
Nothing was too good, too expensive for our
guests, servants of the country. Wine, cigars,
cigarettes, drinks, nothing was missing. We
opened our house, not only to officers, but also
to their relatives who visited them. Our grounds
were enjoyed by many all through the summer.
The house became a sort of high-class hotel
with a homely atmosphere. The servants never
complained about having too much work to do.
Life was intense round those whose duty would
in turn call them to the front.

Many left Thorpe-le-Soken having had as
good a time as was possible to have when not
on duty. Dinners, dances, concerts . . . all
sorts of entertainments took place. Many of
them given with the object of collecting
money for various funds. Arnold always set the
example by giving a substantial subscription.
Rich officers did the same, gladly. The Belgian

Marshal Joffre and Arnold Bennett on the battlefields
of France. The famous Marshal is showing
Arnold Bennett a shell hole in Arras.

Refugees Association, the Red Cross and *La Croix Rouge Française*, all benefited from these efforts. Personally, I felt I was, in my own way, doing all I could to help, as everybody did. I thoroughly enjoyed the part I played as head of the many activities, as manageress and hostess of "Comarques." Arnold was appreciated and admired by all and everyone played up to him, especially women.

In the summer when troops were under canvas we went occasionally to the officers' mess. Arnold disliked going out to tea or dinner anywhere. He kept saying, "You go. I shall not go."

It took me seven years of my married life before I understood that when Arnold said, when invitations were sent to both of us, "Don't think of me. You go and enjoy yourself," he meant it.

I did not care to go without my husband. I was aware that most of the time I was asked because of him. He was the famous one. I was merely his wife and a foreigner. Arnold, to encourage me to go without him, would say, "It is not me they want, it is you." I ended by accepting almost every invitation, realizing that Arnold meant me to do so.

My time was very full and so was his. He wrote all morning, beginning very early.

Happily he never wrote at night. He formed
the habit of going to London every week for
the day—then for a few days. War committees,
war activities called him there. It was a change
for him from "Comarques." He could not have
kept away from London for long . . . from
his clubs, from the glamour of London. He was
highly interested in politics all through the
war. He had to know about politics to some
extent for he was writing for the papers. His
articles were very much sought after. He had
great influence. He was well paid for his
articles. It was a well-known fact. Arnold made
no secret about the price paid to him. In our
part of Essex it was talked about. Once it was
reported to me that a well-known and influential person had spread the rumour that
my husband got huge sums of money for articles
he had no business to write, implying that it
was for "dirty work." I was furious. I was not
in the habit of taking any notice of gossip—far
from it—I always was above gossip. However,
I could not allow such a rumour . . . it was
too serious. It happened that the person accused
of this crime was a friend of mine. I made up
my mind to speak to her when she next came.
I was expecting her for the week-end.

When she arrived I begged her to come into
the drawing-room, and shutting the door, I

asked her to sit down. Then I went straight to the point. "I am sorry to hear the rumour you spread about Arnold's articles on the war and the price paid for them. I want you to help me to contradict such rumours."

"But, Mrs. Bennett, I have said nothing!"

"Suppose you have not, the rumour exists. You must contradict it. I do not mind what you say about myself, my dresses, my going to the mess, etc. I am above all that gossip. It cannot be avoided, but don't you touch my husband's reputation . . . for it will not do."

My friend blushed, apologized and admitted that, after all, she might have innocently referred to the big money Mr. Bennett was earning for his articles, for he had told her himself. After this scene I took my friend to her room.

Our friendship from that day was more secure than ever. She was a great admirer of my husband, after being, at first, afraid of him. She was most amusing and I loved her companionship. She was a great help to me in entertaining our permanent visitors, the officers. With me she went to the officers' mess very often. She joined us when we went to Colchester in my car or to anywhere else. She was great fun and a gossip; but who is not a gossip in a small place?

In her I confided my anxiety about my husband's health. He had not been himself since

his visit to the front. He complained of bad
nights. The slightest noise would wake him.
He insisted that the servants made too much
noise in their bedrooms when going to bed at
night. I told the maids. The noise persisted. I
had extra carpets put on the thick carpets
covering the whole floor of the servants' bedrooms, which were above our own rooms.
Neither my speaking to the maids nor piling
carpets on top of carpets to prevent the noise
made any difference. Arnold in the middle of
the night would leave his bed, and entering my
room, which led from his, would say, making
me jump, "I shall kill those confounded girls
. . . can't you stop them making that noise?"

I would say, "I am so sorry," and crawl out
of my bed and go upstairs and listen. I could
hear no noise nor did I see any light. It was
becoming tragic. Almost every night I was
wakened up that way.

"I wish I could stop that noise," I would
answer.

Arnold would say, "You must."

It occurred to me that, perhaps in my sleep, my
own bed, placed against the wall separating our
rooms, creaked and made this mysterious noise
that Arnold heard so persistently. I changed
my bed from my bedroom to my boudoir.
It made no difference. Arnold had an attack of

'flu. I sent for the doctor, who begged me to make him work less, for his nerves were out of order.

"I wish I could, doctor. It is for you to make him work less . . . tell him so. He will take it from you."

"I doubt it," said the doctor.

I told the doctor about the noises my patient continually heard.

"All nerves, you know. Take no notice."

It was impossible to "take no notice." Nor was it possible to forget that Arnold had a loaded revolver in the drawer of the table by his bed. Who knew what might happen? I thought it wise to unload this toy of his. I ended by asking a man friend, who knew about revolvers, to do it for me. I was to accept the consequences of Arnold's displeasure when he found out. For years the unloaded weapon was in the same drawer by his bed . . . guarding him.

XVIII

ONE day, coming back from London, Arnold said to me, "I have met, for the first time, a most interesting man, Mr. Max Aitken" (afterwards Lord Beaverbrook).

Soon after he said, "Max has asked me to go to Scotland with him in his car. I have accepted."

They went together to Scotland.

Arnold was away for a very long time to my way of thinking, for I was left alone in the house with many people under our roof . . . chiefly men.

Arnold said, "Max is a clever man. He will soon be the richest man and the most powerful in Britain. He came over to England from Canada to conquer England. He is on his way to do so. Should he be Prime Minister one day I wouldn't be surprised. He knows the Prime Minister well. He will be made a lord. He owns *The Daily Express* . . . he is friendly with Rothermere . . . he will one day be the owner of dozens of newspapers. Wait and see. . . . I dare say he sees through me all right!"

These two men, being fully aware of their exceptional gifts, their uncanny cleverness, in

different ways, respected and loved each other
. . . yet both used the other towards his own
ends, as does every business man and philo-
sopher. They had not the same ideas but they
had the same tastes. They loved life, the other
sex, their own amazing popularity. Both had
charm, but while Arnold was a lovable man at
the first meeting, Beaverbrook does not seem
to be so, to the same extent, in the eyes of
many.

His scrutinizing eyes observing you, un-
ostentatiously, his ears missing nothing said
around him, his memory, his uncanny fore-
sight, helped him all through. He has had a
most wonderful life. Arnold was under the
spell of his charm. He was at his service as far
as he approved of what was done. Beaverbrook
squeezed out of him, for the different papers,
Arnold's wonderful brain and talent.

Arnold's reputation as a famous public man
was established before Lord Beaverbrook's.
Arnold, interested in life and human nature,
with the gift of making friends easily at the first
meeting, was bound to get on with a man not
unlike himself in some ways. Both men were
fascinated by society and social gatherings, and
yet reticent and shy when not in the mood for
it. People appealed to them to a certain extent,
but to a greater extent bored them after amus-

ing them for a while. Both born conquerors, both extremely intelligent and broad-minded.

Arnold had not pettiness. He was honest. He only had fads, as geniuses and boys have. He treated everyone in the same way and gave the impression they were necessary to his happiness. There lies the secret of his popularity with his friends. Being a psychologist, he knew how to handle people. To those interested in food, he would draw their attention to food; if interested in other subjects, he would refer to these subjects. He was so much in love with literature that he always ended by talking about books and writing . . . about books, to make his interlocutors interested in them; and in the writing of them, so as to create in any one the desire to write, if only a "journal."

As I have said, he inspired one to make use of one's time, one's energy. Had he invented clocks he could not have loved this material machinery more dearly than he did, for they were the best coach that he knew to teach people to remember their appointments. In his work clocks are often referred to; so are maids' aprons, kitchens and high tea. He wrote *How to Live on Twenty-four Hours a Day, How to Make the Best of Life*, etc., books of essays about everyday things. He knew men's weakness for good food . . . he knew that women knew of

Arnold Bennett at "Comarques"
with one of his French nephews, 1919.

The house "Comarques," Thorpe-le-Soken, Essex.

that weakness. He made the girl in his book, *Helen with the High Hand*, give her miser uncle his favourite dish, kidney omelette, in order to gain her point.

Arnold, though not a miser, liked to handle gold and banknotes. It impressed him to have made the money he handled by the simple means of his knowledge and thoughts put together on blank paper, by the simple process of using a pen moistened with ink.

He knew the value of money as well as the value of time, the value of people. He was always methodical in everything but particularly with his accounts. He did not spend a penny without putting it down. He carried a small pocket-book in his jacket for that purpose, as well as another small book in which to take notes for his work. With the help of his secretary, Miss Nerney, he kept his account books as business men do, up to the end of his consciousness. All the money made was entered into his books; so was the money which was spent. He formed the habit, when undressing to go to bed, of putting his pocket-book, his note-case and his bunch of keys in the drawer of the small table which stood by his bed. Any change he might have in his pocket he put in the chest-of-drawers. I suppose it did not occur to him that some wives might be tempted to lessen, on the

quiet, their husband's belongings. He knew I
would not subtract a farthing from his.

Arnold understood not only money and food,
he understood clothes.

He loved to see women well dressed, well
groomed. He was angry when I used powder,
just to prevent my nose from shining. He would
say, "It takes away your refinement. I hate it."

He used to hate made-up faces or dyed hair.
I am inclined to think that as such artificiality
became fashionable (almost indispensable) he
became used to seeing most of the women that
he admired, in recent years, painted, so that he
ended by liking them better than the unpainted
ones. Mature people and old age appealed to
him. But round fifty he had a decided prefer-
ence for young people. This because he had in
its essence the soul of a naughty child. When
he was about fifty, he confessed to his friend,
E. V. Lucas, that he was beginning to think
young English girls had improved in comparison
with those of the last generation . . . that they
carried their dresses better and were much
better dressed.

Arnold repeated to me what Lucas had said.
"Arnold, it shows you are getting on!"

Like Mr. Prohack, one of his heroes, Arnold
made up his mind to do all in his power to
maintain his youth to the end of his life. He

pretty well succeeded. By the beginning of last February his wonderful vitality was undermined, daily, for seven weeks. Three weeks before the last breath left his body he was unconscious. He, who had all his life the fixed idea he would have a sudden death, a stroke, had to suffer the agony of internal pains; then to realize his will-power was being gradually beaten down, mastered by death calling him away.

He was too ill to ask for anybody but his valet and his secretary. I was anxiously waiting for him to ask for me. Alas! no one suggested to him that I desired to see him, to nurse him. (He used to say, "Marguerite is a born nurse.") Through our deed of separation, though there had never been bitterness between us, I had been asked to give my oath never to enter his home again unless he asked for me.

XIX

THERE is a delightful and true story about my husband. One day he dropped the news on me that he had arranged to go away for three weeks with so and so, and was not taking me.

I said, "What shall I do alone at 'Comarques'? I want to come."

"You can't."

"Why not?"

"Because you can't."

I could not get anything else out of him. I, who all through our married life had never called him names, said in a gentle tone of voice, in French, "*Que tu es chameau!*"

"Am I?" asked Arnold.

"Yes," I said in English to express what I meant. "You are a pig not to take me."

Chameau meaning camel, Arnold was most astonished at being called one. I was not in the habit of teasing him by calling him camel or pig. He was surprised, but said nothing. Three days afterwards he went away from home, leaving me behind. I had not thought twice about calling him a camel, but he had not forgotten. Above the signature of his letter telling me of his happy arrival he had drawn a heart pierced by an arrow—under the heart a tiny camel was standing very straight.

For years his letters to me had, under the signature, the same pierced heart and the same tiny camel standing very straight.

After the war it was my turn to go alone to France. Arnold wrote to me the day I left him. His letter arrived in Paris the same evening. At the end of his letter the unoriginal but faithful pierced heart was drawn, but the camel this time was kneeling in front of the heart. No more camels were drawn on his letters to me from that day! We have never referred to his camels at all.

XX

ARNOLD, like a naughty boy, had to be protected by a feminine hand. Every man needs protection by a woman, just as every child needs his mother's. It is an instinct in woman to protect those she loves. Her protectiveness towards her husband, her brother or her grown-up son, if made obvious, is usually objected to. She has to hide it as if it were a crime. The man, having in a marked degree the instinct of protecting others, resents being protected. He knows that his instinct is also to turn to women, when tired, when heart-broken, when needing comfort. Pride and self-consciousness might lessen this instinct, but there is no such thing as a lover, a husband who loves you, who respects you, who does not ask more or less openly for protection. A married woman is aware of her husband's answer to friends pressing him to do a thing which he does not want to, "I must ask my wife." It follows that wives use, with discrimination or otherwise, the convenient ready-made answer, "I must ask my husband first." Happy are those who can feel wholly protected by those belonging to them, when their protection is needed, either in small things or in large. Women, as a rule, adore it when their protection is called upon. It makes up for neglect. It gives a chance for them to return, in a feeble way, their husbands' all-round protection.

"May I ask you to do something for me?" asked Arnold of me one day, towards the end of the war.

"Of course, my dear. What is it?"

It was not often my husband asked me to do anything for him. He was the one who did things for others when others asked him to do so. It was so unusual for him to ask me to do anything for him that each time it happened I wondered what was up.

This time I was indeed surprised, because up till then he had refused all my invitations, but one, to have a meal with me at my club.

He said, "Marguerite, I would like you to take me to your club one day for lunch. There is a journalist woman coming from America who wants to see me, and I can't avoid it—though I don't want to see her."

"All right. What day am I to ask you two to lunch?"

"I will let you know."

And the day came when I walked from 12 George Street (where we had a flat at the time) to the Empress Club to book a table for three.

143

Arnold, punctual as usual, arrived at the time fixed. He wanted me to know only the name of the woman I was expecting to lunch. A page called out, "Mrs. Arnold Bennett."

I went to meet the journalist guest. She was not young, nor elegant, nor slim, nor *soignée*. I did not like her slack hand-shake. I did not like her. I was prejudiced against her because I knew she had forced herself upon Arnold to the extent that he warned me he was going to leave us together after we had had coffee.

While having lunch we talked about every-day, banal things. I made the conversation go. I could see it was not running in the way this American journalist would have liked. She did not look as if she appreciated either good cooking or the wine served to her. Her mind was not dwelling on the art of cooking nor about the soil producing such nourishment, so necessary to her existence. No! She had come chiefly to be alone with Arnold Bennett, the famous writer, whose articles were read at large and whose influence was great. I was obviously in her way.

"You did not expect that, my girl," Arnold's eyes seemed to say when he looked at her.

He was enjoying the joke. She was red with disappointment.

At the end of lunch I got up, and the three

of us sat in a corner of the lounge. I ordered coffee.

When the waiter left the tray on the round table by us the woman journalist (whose name I do not remember) said, "Well, Mr. Bennett, let us talk about those articles."

"What articles?" said Arnold doggedly.

"You know perfectly well." Her tone seemed to imply "I can't explain in front of this French wife of yours."

"Do you mean about economics and so on?"

"Yes. You should write them."

"I don't want to," said Arnold cuttingly. "Besides, who is going to pay for them?"

The woman looked straight into Arnold's eyes, and said, "You know perfectly where the money comes from."

"Do I?" retorted Arnold. "Anyway, I shall not write these articles you want me to write. I don't believe they will serve any purpose."

"How can you talk like that! . . . It would not be the first one you have written."

"It would, as regards the sort of articles you want."

"I am surprised and disappointed, Mr. Bennett."

She let the matter drop.

I started the conversation again on other subjects and let them carry it on.

My guest said after a while, "Mrs. Bennett, you have not said much, have you?"

"No, I have been listening."

Then I offered her a cigarette.

Arnold rose.

"You must excuse me," he said, "I must leave."

"You can't leave like that. I shall have to see you again."

"I don't think I can manage it," said Arnold.

Fortunately he declared before leaving that he had been delighted to have met her, was sorry he had to leave but pleased he was leaving her in his wife's company.

I was certain my company was not what she had been looking forward to when she came to meet and talk to Arnold Bennett. She in her turn said she had to leave, having an appointment. I saw her to the door of the club.

Shaking hands with me, she said, "I rely on you to make your husband write those articles."

"You know perfectly well he does not want to write them. I will not help him to be caught again in dirty work."

I shall never forget that woman journalist's expression.

The articles were never written.

When, in 1919, Sir H. le Bas's libel action was on, I could not help thinking of this American journalist and of our treatment of her, for my husband's name was brought in front of the public, as well as James Douglas's name, in connection with articles they had been asked to write and had written in the spring of 1918. It was obvious my husband's article was harmless. It was found so. Both men retained their prestige.

The first article, by Arnold Bennett, referred to by Mr. Hogg, was entitled "The Future of Liberalism." It discussed the programme of the Liberal Party. One of the articles by James Douglas was called "A Holiday for Mr. Lloyd George." These articles were written at the time of the question of having a generalissimo and unity of command for the English and French armies.

Arnold was too good a citizen, he was too honest to do anything willingly that was not straight. He was too intelligent not to see when he had been made use of. He did his duty all through the war. He was for two months an efficient Director of the Ministry of Information, which had sprung from Sir H. le Bas's efforts, supported by the Government and backed up by Lord Beaverbrook.

I owe it to Arnold's memory to emphasize the fact that he continually gave up his own work, and that he received no salary while at

the head of the Ministry of Information. He
even had his private secretary to work with him
as a clerk.

Arnold was soon adored by many of the men
in that Ministry. One of them has been his
intimate friend ever since. He made him his
only executor and trustee after joining him in
a theatrical enterprise. His name is Alistair
Tayler.

It is chiefly due to Arnold Bennett, my husband, that the Lyric Theatre, Hammersmith,
taken on a long lease, was a success. For he
soon realized that Nigel Playfair was the
acting manager for such an enterprise, Mr.
Alistair Tayler the right business man, and
he, Arnold, the man whose powerful friends
in the Press would willingly help, for they
had seen for themselves that he was an
extremely efficient man, to be trusted with
money.

The Hammersmith Theatre paid good divi-
dends to shareholders for years. Arnold for a
few years helped by being present at every
meeting and performance, and in giving *le ton*
in every direction. His personality was develop-
ing the personalities of those working in that
theatre. He was made a director only a few
years after the miraculous transformation of a
small theatre in the suburbs into one of the

most fashionable in London. A few years ago he resigned his directorship. I am inclined to think at the end of it all he lost more money in theatrical enterprises than he ever made.

XXI

FROM 1917 up till the end of the war we had convalescent officers staying with us in our country home, "Comarques." Up till 1921 we had some victims of the war staying there with us. It did not prevent us from spending a few days in London each week. We ended by having a large flat, 12 George Street, Piccadilly, and by deciding to spend the winters in London. We could not keep away, after peace was declared, from the active, intellectual life that London has in store for those who seek it.

Arnold, as it was, had decided to drop writing about the Five Towns entirely. It was London he wanted to study . . . in London he was to write. He had in mind many stories, many novels, set in London. His early experiences while in his thirties, and those which in spite of the war he had had, were not a sufficiently rich stock for him to draw from. He had to know more about the activities of London, its inhabitants, the girls, the restaurants, London society and its amusements. He had to see for himself what London cabarets were like, what dancing was like. He who had refused till then to learn dancing felt the need at the age of fifty-two to add this to all his other accomplishments, for it was an art which was greatly in favour during the war and afterwards. The man of fifty-two, who had always hated late nights, began to stay up late, go to suppers, etc.

He was never short of girls anxious to be seen with "Arnold Bennett," whose popularity was great. He was himself most original; he had the gift to make one either laugh or be exasperated . . . constantly to retain attention. He always liked the company of women. No woman meeting him could but be attracted, devoted to him or amused by him. He was out to see what was nice in them and he cleverly pointed it out to them. Women of every age interested him, from seventeen to any age. He was a great favourite with women. This accounted to a great extent for his popularity. He had the same ascendency over men as over women. He was deeply loved by many of them. They were devoted to him. He had, like every artist, an almost feminine mind which appealed to so many. His sense of humour was great. He was more often bored by others than they were bored by him. Frivolity amused him. The sex appealed to him, but he was always on his guard with women.

He hated women's clubs while he loved clubs. He was a member of many. The first

one he joined was the Authors' Club. At the
time his ambition was to become a member
of the Reform Club. After the publication of
his book, *The Old Wives' Tale*, he was made a
member. To him it was a supreme honour. He
adored that club as much as if he had founded
it himself. He adored it so much that he thought
women should not be allowed to enter it. He
hotly refused ever to take me to look over it
for years. It was another member, a friend of
his, who asked me there one day. Arnold was
jealous of his club, of many things, where it
was a question of me, his wife. It was a curious
idiosyncrasy.

Another idiosyncrasy was to refuse to take
me to a public function. I was rarely to be
seen with him at any shows, except theatrical
ones. He was for years asked out alone by
many and he entertained many of his friends
of both sexes in restaurants without me. Then
a friend made him realize the danger of it all
. . . and quietly he confessed he would change
all that. . . . Hence our flat in London and
his desire to start yachting again.

His yacht "Velsa" had been required by the
Admiralty during the war. She had been returned to her owner with a few hundred pounds
for repairs. Arnold added some money to this
sum and had the "Velsa" ready to sail. Soon

afterwards, to my great surprise, he said he had come to the conclusion that he could not afford a flat in town and the "Velsa," so he was contemplating selling her.

"Darling, what about your health? You love the sea and sea air will do you good."

"Never mind," he said.

"You should not sell her," I repeated.

A few weeks afterwards he told me that a member of the Royal Thames Yacht Club had bought her for £1,000.

I exclaimed, "What a bargain for the man and what a pity for you!"

So it was that the "Velsa" went. So it was that the yachting season drew near, and Arnold, tired of London, of a strenuous life, having breakfast with me one fine morning and making my room look bigger and nicer than ever (we were in the habit of having breakfast in my own room), said to me, "You are right, the sea is the thing for me. I think I shall buy myself a yacht."

"If you feel like it, you should. You love it so. You recuperate so when you are at sea."

Arnold explained that he had been told about a yacht which was ready to sail, but he would not give more than he had received for the "Velsa." He loved the yacht offered to him. They wanted over £1,200. He would not accept their price and he ended by going away for a few days to view another yacht. He gave three times as much for her as he had intended. I had the impression that he had been tricked, but I said nothing.

His new yacht was decorated by Lovat Fraser, at the time the designer for the Lyric Theatre, Hammersmith. Arnold did away with all the fittings, bedding, etc. He had a paraffin engine put in. I had to buy fresh linen, china, crockery, etc. Money was lavishly spent on her. She was magnificent. She had a crew of seven men. She was magnificent, and ruinous. I was not without anxiety. Arnold's conscience was not at peace, though his fancy was satisfied. I loved to see him excited about his new toy . . . his new hobby.

He was aware, when he was suffering from nervous headaches and general depression, that I was thinking about the possibility that he would not be able to carry on and of the tragedy of us, especially of him, reduced almost to poverty. He could read my thoughts in my face at all times. "Security should be one of your objects, my love," my expression would reveal to him when I nursed him or sat by his bedside.

It was on one of these occasions that he said to me in a serious tone of voice, "You are my own conscience. Do you think it is easy to live in front of one's own conscience?"

I was confounded. But I knew he knew I had the better balanced mind of the two. I knew that he had acknowledged that with me he would never be ruined. He knew in his conscience that my moderation in everything was a good thing for us both. But one cannot change anybody nor influence them for long. I ended by accepting what could not be helped, his extravagance, and I made no remark about the risk of spending too much. Arnold made the money and he had the first claim on it. I relied on his commonsense for the security of his old age, for he was a business man and dreaded poverty.

His yacht had a name that he disliked. He could not decide what name to give her, so he told our household when he came back to "Comarques" for the week-end.

We had at the time two of my own young relatives staying with us and also a victim of the war. Arnold was, like me, interested in youths and, like me, loved to give others a good time. These young relations of mine had come over to learn English, but they only spoke French to me and to "Uncle Arnold." Arnold, who loved speaking French, found in these boys a sort of relaxation from his strenuous week in London. He loved to play the father with them, as well as the brother, the schoolmaster.

He had no difficulty in making these boys interested in his expensive toy, the new boat.

"*Avez-vous une photo de votre yacht, mon oncle?*"

"*Oui, mes enfants,*" and the boys were excited when the photos of Arnold's new boat were shown to them.

"*Comment l'appelez-vous, mon oncle?*" they asked.

"Suppose you help me to find a name for her."

My Christian names were suggested. Their uncle answered, "Marie Marguerite is no doubt a beautiful name."

It was left at that, but soon afterwards the boys asked their uncle, "Have you decided about the new name for your magnificent yacht, uncle?"

"Not quite," said Arnold, looking at me.

"It would be nice for you, *ma tante*, if *mon oncle* were to call her after you."

"All right, my boys, I will," said their uncle.

I was very flattered. It was the first time my husband had honoured me publicly. He had up till then refused to dedicate any book to me on the basis that he did not believe in husbands dedicating books to their wives.

Arnold Bennett on board his yacht "Marie Marguerite."

The day before Arnold's yacht was christened I joined my husband at Brightlingsea. He, the skipper and one of the crew came to fetch me in the dinghy. On it was painted the name, "Marie-Marguerite." A long name. On the men's sweaters was written the same double name, embroidered in a curve and covering the whole breast. Who would not have been proud to be the owner's wife and to see her own name written everywhere on the ship, the dinghy and on the crew's jerseys? I was the god-mother of the "Marie-Marguerite" and I christened her.

My stay on her did not last long, for duty called me back to our country home.

Arnold had that summer a long list of friends who had accepted his invitation to cruise with him. He was away on the "Marie-Marguerite" all that summer and the following one of 1921. He entertained lavishly. He had a gramophone and used to watch his guests dancing . . . he had a happy time.

Meanwhile, I was at "Comarques" with visitors and far from well with worry and re-sponsibilities.

I was deprived of my husband's company all through the summer, except for a few days.

On the 15th September, 1921, I joined him, bringing with me a girl friend whom he had invited. This, I must confess, displeased me immensely. I did so much want to have at least a fortnight alone with him before we went back to our flat in London for the winter.

I do not know, and I shall never know, whose influence my dear husband was under at that time, but I know that our life together became more and more difficult. He had begun to tire of our country home, "Comarques." He wanted to sell it. I was attached to that house more than I can explain. It thoroughly upset me. I felt it was my duty towards him and myself to do all in my power to prevent what was, in my eyes, a real catastrophe. In my efforts to prevent him from selling the house I was backed up by the father and mother of the French boys, my relatives. We came to no final conclusion about "Comarques" while at Ostende.

I preceded my husband to London so as to have the flat ready on his return.

We had had some invitations and we had arranged also to start a poetry society. Arnold was president. Miss Edith Sitwell, Miss Helen Rotham and myself formed the committee.

I was the chief interpreter of the French poems on the programme. It was work I adored, giving me scope for self-expression. I loved the work of Verlaine and Baudelaire— two of our great French poets.

Another meeting took place, this time at

Lord and Lady Swaythling's, at the end of October. Two days afterwards, as a result of a misunderstanding with my husband, I was asked, to my great surprise, by our solicitors, to leave our flat at once, for the sake of Arnold's work. I obeyed like an ignorant fool and I was never allowed to return to it. There was no judicial separation, but a deed of separation was drawn.

We have lived apart ever since. To me, years of intense loneliness and suffering. . . . Childless, handicapped by name instead of being helped by it, I have filled all these long years by looking after my friends' children, as I had always done when I realized, soon after we were married, that we should have no children of our own. I have also kept my journal, published a short biography of my husband (in 1925), and written a few books (unpublished). I was encouraged in my effort by the fact that Arnold was the first to say I could write.

I think my husband came to the conclusion, after a while, that our separation was a great mistake, but circumstances overwhelmed him . . . he was in love with life, not with security.

We felt no resentment, but I have always felt, and I still claim, that our separation was a great mistake which could have been easily avoided if other people had minded their own business and if my husband had not been an influential man that people played up to. In marriage one must give and take, and more especially with independent, mature people in love with life, as we were.

Those around us, knowing us both, were well aware that, fundamentally speaking, Arnold and I were born for each other. That has been pointed out by a famous writer who appreciated us, knew us both well and knew what he was talking about—Hugh Walpole.

He knew my anxiety when Arnold was ill and overworked . . . worn out by so many people asking for his help. How anxious I was lest I should lose him. How I tried to keep cheerful, for Arnold hated long faces. How lonely I felt so often. . . . I was puzzled at Arnold going to London so often, after the way he had appreciated our home, "Comarques." How distressed I was trying to find a way to gain my husband's confidence. The difficulty I had to persuade him to see a doctor. How I arranged with a friend he should see one, whether he liked it or not.

Arnold was by nature a bachelor. He was, then, unconsciously striving to regain his freedom . . . if only for a time. Personally, I have hated my freedom, not wanting to make use of it. I have had a home in London and all these years I have followed the wonderful progress of Arnold's success up till the end. I have heard from him every quarter, when sending my allowance (not fixed by law, but by himself of his own free will), and when writing to me at Christmas and on my birthday without fail.

Can I believe Arnold no longer loved me? I cannot . . . and death has taken him away!

Many have felt his departure. In France he had many friends. He loved France. When French writers or musicians came to England and were introduced to Arnold they soon became his friends. He helped many.

I remember a visit a well-known French writer, Valery Larbaud, paid us in London. I cannot remember exactly how he happened to know I kept my "Journal" (possibly because I had shown him Arnold's wonderful manuscripts —I used to show them to our visitors who were likely to be interested). He had possibly also noticed the beautiful blue morocco binding, not unlike some of Arnold's . . . anyway he asked me (when Arnold left us after lunch) if he might take my "Journal" and read it.

I exclaimed, "I am not sure!"

He opened the manuscript. I looked at the page he had opened it at and said, "You may read that, if you like!"

When Arnold had left he had said good-bye to Larbaud, for he—Larbaud—had to catch a train. When Arnold came back after tea Larbaud was in the drawing-room standing by a book-case reading my "Journal."

"I did not expect to see you again," Arnold remarked. Then noticing the blue binding, he said, "Oh! you are reading my wife's 'Journal' . . . you are sure to miss your train."

"I am afraid so. Rather interesting," replied Larbaud.

"There is not a word of truth in it," said Arnold, with a wink.

I laughed.

XXII

IF he were alive and near me he might come beside my chair while I am writing the last lines on this manuscript (a token of my love, my appreciation, and my admiration for him) and might say, "There is not a word of truth in it." And again I would laugh.

I would say to him, "Darling, shall I add that, in common with the poet, Charles Baudelaire, you enjoyed my tears when you were the cause of them? . . . You were sure then of my love for you, great lover of life! Have you ever realized to what an extent I belong to you? I shall not attempt to describe or criticize your work. . . . I leave that to others."

Rest in peace, and let me quote this poem, written on your death by a psychologist, an admirer of yours—a woman unknown to me and to many of her readers.

"A MAN FROM THE NORTH"

Enoch Arnold Bennett, 1867-1931

Here lies a man, from common clay descended,
  Who took the common people of the clay
And from their lives of grime and greatness
    blended
  Created Life that shall not pass away.

Here lies a child who penned with childish
    pleasure
  The pageantry before his eyes unfurled,
The pomps and shows, the luxury and leisure,
  The gauds and glitter of the rich man's world;

Yet still could sing, with sympathy unblunted,
  With understanding welded doubly sure,
The saga of the straitened and the stunted,
  The patience and the pathos of the poor.

Here lies a sage who saw in things material
  The outward workings of some cosmic plan—
Each day a chapter in some breathless serial
  Written by Fate for the delight of Man.

MY ARNOLD BENNETT

Here lies a jester with a sense of duty,
   A master-craftsman in his craft engrossed,
A steadfast friend, a worshipper of beauty,
   A kindly critic and a perfect host.

Here lies, in fine, a connoisseur of living
   For whom adventure lurked in every breath;
Shall not his soul go forth without misgiving
    To greet the Great Adventure which is
    Death?

[*By kind permission of the Proprietors of "Punch."*]

LONDON,
Sunday, 31st May, 1931

The Westminster Press
411A Harrow Road
London, W.9